Get Into Property

Go from Property Beginner to Property Expert

by David Siegler

Get Into Property by David Siegler
www.davidsiegler.co.uk

Design by Luke Bunting
Research by David Siegler
© Copyright 2019 David Siegler

Note for Librarians: A cataloguing record for this book is available from Library and Archives Canada at www.collectionscanada.gc.ca/a-z-index/ index-e.html

Printed in Peterborough, Cambridgeshire, UK ISBN: 978-1909846-58-6

Published by Progressive Publishing
Progressive House
Units 8, 9 & 10
Cygnet Park, Forder Way, Hampton Peterborough, PE7 8GX

Email: info@davidsiegler.co.uk
Facebook: www.facebook.com/DavidSieglerInvestments

READ THIS

Hi there, firstly a big thank you for purchasing your copy of Get Into Property: Go from property beginner to property expert.

This book will show you the building blocks to success and how you can go from a property novice to a expert property investor. You will learn the fundamentals of property investing as well as the strategies you need to maximise cashflow.

I hope to have covered as much as I can into this book BUT the property market moves fast and I constantly have more I want to share with you to keep you one step ahead of the rest.

That's why I have created an online resource. This online resource will help keep you up to date with the latest and hottest property strategies and give you a competitive advantage over other property investors.

To get immediate access to your bonus gift — go here now before you continue reading:

🔍 **www.getintoproperty.co.uk**

David Siegler

Contents

PART ONE: GETTING STARTED

Chapter One: "What Do You Mean,
The House Is On Fire?" 17

    i)   How It Started 17

    ii)   How Things Have Changed 18

Chapter Two: Who Is This Book For? 25

Chapter Three: Setting Out: Why Are You
Thinking Of Buying And Flipping Houses? 27

Chapter Four: Life Is Different In 2019 31

Chapter Five: A Shortcut To Earning Big Money 33

Chapter Six: Why Listen To Me? 35

Chapter Seven: Flippin' Houses 41

    i)   How Do You Start? 41

    ii)   What I Did Wrong 42

Chapter Eight: So Where Should You Buy? 45

Chapter Nine: What To Buy? 51

Chapter Ten: What Are You Looking For?
What Is A Deal? 57

    i)   Gross Yield And Stacking The Deal 58

Chapter Eleven: Should You Buy In The North Or The
South? A Perspective Based On Experience Of Both ... 61

    i)   Squaring The Circle 66

Chapter Twelve: Putting Your Power Team Together .. 69

Chapter Thirteen: Builders 73

Chapter Fourteen: Flippin' Builders 79

Chapter Fifteen: Sourcing The Deal 89

Chapter Sixteen: Viewing The Houses 91

Chapter Seventeen: Sourcing The Deal – Auctions ... 101

    i)   Chief Executive Officer In Charge Of Auction Acquisitions 108

Chapter Eighteen: Flip To Auction - Selling In Auction 113

    i)   Buy, Don't Refurb, Sell 114

    ii)   Conditional Offers 120

Chapter Nineteen: Funding The Deal 131

i) Bank Of Mum And Dad 131

ii) Joint Venture Finance 132

iii) Attracting Investors To Finance Your Flips 135

iv) Face-To-Face Meetings 137

v) Recommendations And Referrals 148

vi) Finding Investors Online 149

vii) Bridging Finance 157

Chapter Twenty: How To Price A Refurb 159

Chapter Twenty-One: Refurbish, Don't Renovate 167

Chapter Twenty-Two: Setting Up Your First Investment Property And Your First Tenant 169

PART TWO: MY STORY

Chapter Twenty-Three: Show Me The Money (Part 1) 175

i) Why Get Into Packaging Deals? 175

ii) What This Is Not 177

iii) What This Is 180

Chapter Twenty-Four: Moving Forward 185

Chapter Twenty-Five: Doing Some Deals 191

Chapter Twenty-Six: Scaling Up 195

i) Going Wholesale 197

Chapter Twenty-Seven: Building A Business 205

Chapter Twenty-Eight: Compliance 207

i) What Do You Need? 208

Chapter Twenty-Nine: Show Me The Money (Part 2)   215

i) Finder's Fee 216

ii) Pre-Packaged Deal 219

iii) Searching For Bigger Fees 224

Chapter Thirty: Just Flippin' Do It 229

Foreword by Sheryl Siegler

"I do love him but…
…it wasn't always like that".

I was minding my own business, dancing around my handbag at the "Fresher's Ball" at Leicester University, in the Autumn of 1974. That was the first time I spotted David Siegler. I had no idea that over the next 44 years or so, he would play (and continue to play) such a huge role in my life.

To be fair, he was a bit of a strange sight at the time. I remember he was wearing jeans with huge flared bottoms, in two tone purple and black as was the fashion at the time. From memory he was a bit taller than he is today, but maybe that's just because his 30-inch flares concealed 3-inch platform shoes which he appeared to fall off on a regular basis. I remember him on that life changing evening, dancing in a strange, but cool and groovy kind of way (or so he seemed to think). He also sported shoulder length hair which broke in a tousled manner, slightly below the shoulder line of his very tight-fitting shirt. He has always struggled with tight-fitting shirts even to this day. They don't really suit him and he doesn't have the build for them. I could never bring myself to share this with him directly though!

What a pair we must have looked later that week as we set out on our first date. It was a strange date. I had to push his car, an elderly Ford Anglia with a Mickey Mouse sticker on the bonnet, in the snow when he came to pick me up. I then had to push it again at the end of the date when he offered to take me home. In between I saw very little of him as he had to keep rushing off to the loo, having been struck down by some dreadful, student-like tummy upset. He did manage to summon the strength to check in with me briefly every 20 minutes or so, presumably to see if I was still there.

And so we set off on our incredible adventure, one that has continued to this day.

I need to share with you a little about the property bit too, since that's presumably why you're reading. We've learned a lot together but when we started out we were probably a lot like you; we knew that we could make some money from property but we didn't know how to start.

The first property we bought was a shop in 1977. This was followed a year later by another shop. David was a retailer at that time and we bought the shops in order to earn some money. The second shop had two floors of rooms above, which remained empty for 20 years before we converted them into three apartments. We rented the apartments out to increase the yield on the property and still rent them out today. In the early days we knew so little about maximising return in property that it took us 20 years to do it.

We bought out first home in 1982. It was the most expensive house on the street on the day we bought it, the grand sum of £35,995. We had borrowed £27,000 from the Alliance Building Society as it was, and the first payments were made at a rate of 16%. We felt so fortunate to get the mortgage back then. How times have changed.

Moving forward to 2019, we have somehow managed to accumulate interests in property that provide us with an income of several thousands of pounds every month. The equity in those properties is significant, more than £2,500,000 now and growing every year. There is also the income David has produced in his sourcing and packaging business where he has placed over 250 deals with investors.

Property has given us the freedom to live the life that we want to live, and I know that you want that too.

So, here is my advice to you:

Read this book. Do what David tells you to do. We have been through so much over the years, made our mistakes and had to fix them along the way. David will help you avoid the pitfalls while at the same time helping you to move forwards and build your legacy.

This is the story of our experiences in flipping houses. I hope that you set out on your way to build a big property portfolio and I wish you all the fun, joy and success that we have enjoyed on our journey.

Turn the page, it's time to get started.

Acknowledgements

With love to Sheryl Siegler. The smartest, kindest and most supportive woman I have ever met. I have no idea how my life would have turned out if we had not met on that fateful day in 1974. I will love you always.

To Rob Moore and Mark Homer. Two of the smartest and most supportive men that I have ever met. I would not be doing what I love today without your encouragement and support. Thank you both.

PART 1: GETTING STARTED

Chapter One: "What Do You Mean, The House Is On Fire?"

How It Started

This was to be a big day for my business partner DG, and myself. A huge day in our property business. We had been waiting for this for a really, really long time. We had made a false start, in fact we'd made several false starts, but for the very first time we had managed to get an investor, Martin, who had shown interest in working with us. We were going to do the rounds with the estate agents in and around our home ground of Oldham in Greater Manchester. This had been a long time coming.

We'd first gone to Manchester, or rather I had first gone to Manchester in 2004. I really didn't want to go. You see, I live in Brighton, which is a lovely place on the South Coast of England but Manchester is up North. I'd never been. I had seen it on the TV and I thought it was a bit ugly looking. I didn't really want to go but my business partner was committed to the area because his daughter had been a student at Manchester University. She'd completed a degree course there, she'd lived there four years and at the end of her studies she decided that she had found her life-partner there. She had fallen in love and she wanted to stay on and build a life there with her new found love.

So what DG did, was he rented a house for her in Ashton-under-Lyne. She stayed on in Greater Manchester and moved in with her new partner. Unfortunately, the love affair did not last but I digress.

My business partner went up and stayed for a weekend and he and Mrs DG did the parent weekend thing, visiting with his daughter and her new partner. You know what's it like, you go and meet the families and all that sort of stuff. At some point, he was in the house that he had rented for the love-struck couple and was reading the local paper.

He knew he was paying £400 a month to rent this house for his daughter and her then boyfriend, but he saw in the newspaper that he could buy the house next door for £35,000 at that time. The arithmetic was pretty compelling. The girls went shopping in the city for handbags, shoes or whatever else. DG, my business partner also went shopping, but to the estate agents. He bought a house, and then he carried on buying more houses, because life was very different then.

In those days, lack of finance was not a problem. You could raise finance easily. Finance was very available. You could get a Buy-to-Let mortgage anywhere. I remember from my own records at the time I recorded over 130 lenders in the market on a particular day, all of them eager to provide a Buy-to-Let mortgage to anyone who might be casually passing by, looking to borrow £200k or maybe even £300k.

How Things Have Changed

So DG went off and bought houses. And then bought some more houses. He used to come home to Brighton, and he would say to me "You ought to come and have a look at this." I was initially pretty reluctant, and my typical response would be "No, it's not for me. I don't really want go. It's quite a long way away. I've seen it on the TV. It looks a bit grubby. I would rather stay here. I'm not going to do it."

Eventually DG persuaded me.

A couple of weeks later he picked me up in the car and I complained all the way up the M6 motorway. We wandered from the carpark into Ashton-under-Lyne, the small town in Greater Manchester where we were looking to buy property and it took me about 45 minutes to get into the swing of it.

One of our first calls was to a really old, established estate agent in Ashton-under-Lyne. They are still there to this day. At the time it was a big double fronted shop with a door in the middle. We went in to have a look, see what they had in their window, on their display shelves and in their property books. If we were lucky, we hoped we may even get a look at what they had off-market. You know, those properties not yet marketed but tucked away in one of their secret drawers for their special investor clients.

As we approached the front door, two gentlemen rolled out onto the pavement and appeared to be having a fist fight. We couldn't really understand what was happening, but we carefully walked around them, went into the shop and asked "What's going on?"

"Well, the gentleman underneath has just bid £40,000 for a house, and the gentleman on top came in and bid £41,000. They've just stepped outside to sort it out privately between them."

This was in 2004. It was a sign that the market was heating up but it's not an economic indicator that you'll see on the news at ten or any financial analysis programme on the television; be aware.

"This looks like fun," I thought. "This is something that I might enjoy."

I hung around and we started buying houses, and then we carried on buying more houses. Then we started buying them like they were Kit Kats, because you could raise mortgages in 2004. Anyone could raise mortgages in 2004. You could raise mortgages on the phone, you just had to put deposits in. You could even self-certify that you were in a position to pay the money back.

I know it's unthinkable now, but that is what happened and it's no great surprise that everything changed after the financial crisis of 2008.

Back in 2004, you just put your deposit in, bought a house with a mortgage, and in a rapidly rising property market you could quickly refinance and get most of your money out and go again. That was how a lot of people started out in property at that time.

You always had to leave a little bit of money in, and you never got it all out, but that's how it worked. The problem is that if you are funding it all yourself, then over a period of time you eventually have all of your money for deposits tied up, and you run out of further deposits. This was a problem.

Soon we came up with another plan. We decided that for every two or three houses that we bought to add to our portfolio, we would find another that we could buy, add some value to, and then sell again for a profit. It was a flip. I didn't even know it was called a flip at the time, but that is what we did.

If you're already a property person, you'll know that it doesn't matter what you do. Whatever your strategy is, however quickly you can turn around your flips, you will run out of money at some point. Eventually we ran out of money.

Over that time, we'd been really busy. We had built all these fantastic contacts. We had been going up to Manchester every week and we had been buying every week. We had been viewing every week and had built an army of contacts who were bringing us leads. All of these estate agents and others were showing us houses, bringing us properties and telling us about opportunities. We really valued the contacts that we made, although some of them were a little unconventional and exotic as you will hear later. This network was the heart and soul of our business.

What we couldn't bring ourselves to say to any of them, was:

"No. we're really sorry. We can't make you an offer for the next one. In fact, we've run out of money, and it's probably going to be a year before we can buy anything again."

You know what would happen if we said that, right? We wouldn't get any more offers. We wouldn't get any more opportunities to buy. We would lose the network that we had built.

So we asked ourselves, could we get someone else to buy the houses that we no longer had the funds to buy and could we earn any money from that? That was the thought process. We didn't really know what we were doing at the time, or even if that was a feasible idea. It just seemed the next logical thing to do in our circumstances.

We had started to talk socially about what we were doing and it seemed that fate was on our side because at the time there was a big hunger from all sorts of people who wanted to buy houses. Anyone who had a few thousand pounds wanted to get on the property ladder. There were related programmes every day on TV, and property became a way of life for many people. They wanted to increase their wealth and build their legacy. I had all sorts of people approaching me in Brighton who made it very clear that they had a few pounds tucked away and that might like to buy a couple of "cheap" houses "up North" if we had any going spare.

It is hard now, in 2019 to remember how different the world was before the financial crash. It was relatively inexpensive to get on the property ladder at that point, and as I've mentioned, finance was plentiful. In fact, it was abundant and everywhere; raising mortgages was not difficult to do.

We came back every weekend to Brighton, which was (and still is) an expensive area in which to buy property. We told people about what we were doing in the North West of England, a low cost area to buy property. The decision to invest was a no-brainer for them. They were all-in and they were all over it. Anyone with say, £5,000 as a deposit could buy a house at that time. There were many opportunities in the North West of England at around £50,000 in reasonable areas, and there were lenders who would only need a 10% deposit from the investor. Some of the people who wanted to buy didn't even have the £5,000 in cash! It wasn't unusual for them to raise the money for a deposit on a credit card. This is unthinkable today but was mainstream just those few years ago.

I had all sorts of people from all walks of life approaching me because they wanted to buy cheap houses in the North of England. There were taxi drivers and dentists, professional sportsmen and the self-employed business owners. Basically anyone and everyone was in on the opportunity.

"Those houses that you are buying up North, David, do you have any spares? Maybe a couple of old ones that you don't want?" they would say. I never really understood what that meant, since they were largely all Victorian terraced properties; they were all old!

In this book I am going to take you on the journey that I went through from virtual beginner to getting to the position where I had a thriving property business. I started out by just wanting to buy a few houses as an investment that over time might provide wealth and prosperity for my family. Maybe you are a virtual beginner who would like to provide more for your family? I will show you how.

My journey led to me getting involved in flipping houses to generate big chunks of cash to keep the whole show on the road. Maybe you would like to learn how to generate big chunks of cash through flipping houses so that you have the money you need in your life? I will show you how.

Later in this book I will show you how, as you earn and learn, you can pick up skills in the world of property that can make you self-sufficient and financially free. Through applying these skills, you may never have to do another day's work again in your life if you don't want to. Even more significantly perhaps, I'll show you how you can go through the process of learning how to be an investor, how to flip properties to generate cash, and even how you can flip properties to earn cash without having to buy them in the first place. You won't need any finance, deposits or joint venture loans. In fact, you don't need any money at all. I went through the process and pain of learning how to do this. I will show you how.

Stay with me.

In sharing that backstory, I'm afraid I got a little distracted, but I need to go back to Martin. Remember him? He was the very first investor that came up to Manchester with us to see what we were doing.

We picked him up at the railway station and whisked him away out to our patch. We went into the very first estate agents' office that we were going to visit that day. It was the local office of Ryder & Dutton. They are still there today, quite a big regional firm in the North West of England. I was in the office greeting my estate agent friends who were working there at that time, when I overheard some terrible and chilling words. I didn't quite digest them at first but they soon sank in and a shudder ran down my spine. "What do mean the house is on fire?", I heard Martin say into his phone.

Well, it turns out that his house, his home, back in the South of England was on fire. His wife was on the phone breaking this terrible news to him. She had been doing laundry and the tumble dryer had caught alight while it was in cycle. She hadn't been aware, and hadn't been in the room to notice. The house was filled with smoke and there was a fire. The fire brigade had come and everyone was safe, but the house was severely damaged.

As you'd expect, this became something of a distraction. It took Martin's focus away from the business in hand, the business we had planned, that he might buy a house or two off us that particular day so that we could earn some fees. Instead, he needed to return home urgently.

Never mind how Martin felt; I was devastated. This was a huge blow for me. I would not be earning any money that week, and it was a lesson. It was a lesson that I will share with you later on.

Martin got home, and everything was resolved. He and his family had to live in rented accommodation for about nine months while the house was being put back to pristine condition, and everybody lived happily ever after. There was a massive insurance claim and the insurance company honoured their responsibility, so that was all good.

However, the insurance company didn't care about me. They didn't care how carefully we had cultivated Martin's interest in what we were doing over a long period of time. They didn't care that we had finally got Martin to come up to Manchester to see what we were doing. They didn't care that we were going to attempt to sell him some houses. They didn't care that these were going to be our very first deal packaging fees.

He had stayed in the town for about seven minutes; that's how long he'd been on our patch with us. We didn't get a chance to show him anything. We picked him up from the railway station, and shortly after, ran him back to the railway station.

That was the start of my deal packaging career. In the second half of this book I'm going to share with you how you can start your own deal packaging business too. I'll share how you get from that starting point, where you have no deals, no investors, a virtual car crash, a fire sale in the middle of Ashton-under-Lyne and no fees and no business in the pipeline, through to where you can build a business in your time, on your terms, that can generate a six figure income for you each year. Let me explain who this book is targeted at.

Chapter Two: Who Is This Book For?

This book is going to be for those of you who want to earn life-changing money through property. It is for those of you who want to earn enough money that you can have the freedom, the time, the choice and everything you want in your life. I believe that we all come into property **a)** to build a property portfolio, but **b)** so that that property portfolio can generate money. The money allows us to spend time doing what we love, sharing special moments with our loved ones, going on holidays and being together. No longer are we stuck working in the nine-to-five world. Instead we are working on our own terms and building our own dreams.

That is what property is about, and I'm going to show you how you can do that. It doesn't really matter how much money you are looking to make from property. Maybe you are an empire builder? Maybe you are someone who wants to build a really big property business? If you're reading this book as someone who wants to work a 100 hours per week and build yourself a massive business, turning over seven figures a year then this book is for you. This book will give you the foundations you need to set out on that journey.

Maybe though, what you want is for your property investments to serve you. Maybe you are not really looking to build a huge empire, but instead what you want is for your life to be funded by the property investments that you make so that you have the time to do whatever in life it is that you want to do. That might be just having more free time; time to spend with loved ones, time to travel, time to give back, time to smell the roses along the way.

Whatever it is you are looking for this book will help you to become financially secure so that you can achieve it.

If you want a million-pound business, or if you want the choice and freedom to live your life how you want to, let's get on with it, let's dive straight in at the deep end. One thing I can promise you is that this is not going to be difficult. This is going to be easy. I'm going to talk more about that in the next chapter.

Chapter Three: Setting Out: Why Are You Thinking Of Buying And Flipping Houses?

Property brings wealth. Property can set you free.

You can become a millionaire by investing in houses. Even if you don't know much about the strategies of property as a business then one thing can be guaranteed; if you buy a house, even if you do nothing at all with it, even if you don't do it up, even if you don't rent it out, it will still make you money. If all you do is just keep it long enough then, over time, the ownership of that house will make you wealthy.

I have experienced this phenomenon myself. In 1985 I bought a house which cost £91,000. At the time I could only raise a mortgage of £50,000 so I needed another £41,000 to complete the purchase. I didn't have the money but I begged and borrowed it and made it over the line. I still own that house today. It still has a £50,000 mortgage on it because I have re-mortgaged it a couple of times over the years. I was recently thinking of selling up so I had it valued for sale. It is no longer worth £91,000 but is instead worth £910,000. When I share that with non-property people for the first time, I sometimes hear some "Ooohs" and a few "Aaaahs" in the background. The thing is, this massive growth is not about me. It's nothing to do with me. I've done nothing clever to generate it. I've done nothing, all I have done is to get older.

The point is that over time property can make you wealthy.

Returning to my back-story, you'll recall that we had journeyed up the M6, two "soft southerners" set to make their fortune in the North of England where the streets are paved with gold. But where would we start?

We had a plan. In fact, we had two different plans and I will share my plan with you now.

My plan was very simple. It was based upon the accepted wisdom of property investors, forged over the ages. That accepted wisdom is that property prices double every ten years. Based on that premise I went to work armed with a plan which was that I wanted to put together a portfolio of houses which would produce a cash-flow after all costs, of £4,000 per calendar month (pcm). Looking at property values and rent demand in this particular area at the time, I estimated that ten houses, unencumbered by debt would result in this cash-flow. This was where the plan got really clever.

In order to accumulate ten houses unencumbered by debt, if property prices double every ten years, then what I needed to do was to purchase 20 houses using mortgages. Over ten years they would double in value so I could sell half of them which would pay off the mortgages on all of them. Then I would be left with ten unencumbered houses producing the required £4,000 pcm. That's a solid plan, right?

Of course, we all know about the oft-quoted rule of thumb that property prices double every ten years. To be fair, there have been periods over the centuries when this law has been made to look a little shaky. In some parts of the country, this has been the case within the last ten years. However, we can track the growth in property prices going back to the Norman Conquest, and if we do so then we discover some quite surprising results.

On Boxing Day 1088, Good King William sent out his tax official with instructions to assess and value the worth of all the property in England and Wales. All the calculations were to be included in a great book which was to become known as The Doomsday Book, copies of which we can still study and refer to today. At that time, the powers-that-be decided to exclude London from the census, for reasons that I don't know. Scotland was also excluded. You have to remember that times were very different then and King William and his advisors thought that the Tax Assessors might not fare too well if they journeyed to Scotland. Back then, Scotland was virtually an independent country and didn't take too kindly to interference in its affairs from a distant government based in London. It was considered that things might be a bit lively for the Tax Assessors if they strayed north of Hadrian's Wall. That was nearly 1000 years ago; maybe not too much has changed since?!

Another place where the tax assessors might not have been expected to do well may have been in Hastings. Now Hastings is a place where, on the face of it, King William had one of the major successes of his career and of his life? In truth he had not really done too well in Hastings since taking power back in 1066. At the time, the area around Hastings was heavily forested and the local community lived in the woods. I think it's fair to say that they enjoyed their own company and did not take well to strangers.

When the Normans arrived on the beaches at Hastings in 1066, the local community were ready. They knew the Normans were coming and they hid in the woods with their faces painted in blue woad. Every now and again they would peek out and make the Normans feel very unwelcome with their various cries and chants and yah-boo faces. In that era the Normans were an awesome and formidable fighting machine and they had won many battles against many fearsome foes across Europe. They feared no-one. They were not easily unsettled, but when they looked at the terrain and in particular, the lively welcome that might be in store for them from the local "Haystingers" (as they were known), even the Normans had second thoughts. They thought about it and decided that on this occasion perhaps discretion would be the better part of valour. Under the circumstances they decided to take a detour around Hastings and continued on to London without troubling the locals. In fact, even the Battle of Hastings was not in Hastings but several miles down the road towards Bexhill.

King William and his entourage had never been back to "parlez" with the Haystingers since that day and it's fair to assume that relationships between the Normans and the locals were likely to be a bit strained. Untroubled by that, Norman tax inspectors were duly dispatched to Hastings in order to make their assessment.

They never returned, and no-one knew what happened to them. No-one else was sent down to Hastings to attempt to do the job again. And that is why Hastings is the only town in England that existed at the time of the census, but was not included in the Doomsday Book.

The total value of all the land and property that was counted in England and Wales at the time, came to approximately £1million. Now, 1,000 years later there are thousands of properties in the UK today which individually have a value in excess of £1million. Things have moved on. The point of all this history, is to demonstrate that over time, the value of property in the UK doubles roughly every 10 years. I believe there might even be an EU directive in place to that effect if we look closely enough.

Personally, I don't believe it matters when you start buying and flipping property as long as you do start. Over the time that I have been a property investor there have been at least three property booms and then three property crashes. Prices go up, prices go down. If you hang on in there, prices ALWAYS recover and then go on rising to reach new, unthinkable heights. So you should start today. If prices drop a little bit in the next 12 months, then just grin and bear it. You'll be fine.

In 25 years' time, the numbers will have outperformed all your expectations and you won't even remember the stress of the first year in the game.

Chapter Four: Life Is Different In 2019

Although you now hopefully understand the power of capital growth over time to change your lifestyle and your life, what if this is not your primary concern today? What if you need (I mean, really, really need) more income in your life?

Society is constantly changing. What worked for our parents, will not necessarily work for us. In the old days if you needed more money then you just went and got a second job. You worked harder and longer. That was how my parents did it and possibly that is how your parents did it also. Unfortunately, I don't believe that this can work today. The problem in my view, is caused by inflation over time and the reduction in value of wages. Wages have not kept pace with asset price rises over time, and no matter how many hours you work you cannot work for enough hours to earn what you need to earn. This is one reason why we perceive that the rich have got richer; they don't spend their time working longer and longer hours. Instead, they learn how to invest in assets that rise in value over time.

I accept that you still need a larger income today and you need it now. For a young family in the UK today it is really difficult to provide what you need to provide, to have all the material things that you believe you should have access to if there is only one income coming into a household. The prices of all the gadgets and stuff that we actually need in our lives today is too high.

The challenge is compounded if you're a parent. As a parent, you deserve to have time with your kids and family. What is the point of bringing children into the world if you have to spend all your waking hours in various jobs full-time and part-time and never see the kids? You may struggle to have the time to guide them and teach them and help them grow into the adults they should be. That was presumably not the plan when you decided to start a family? To meet the demands for income to meet your needs, and to free up your time, what you need are multiple streams of income. You need income generating activities and assets in your life that will produce the money you need without dragging you away too much from the things in your life that you want to do.

I want to help you to access these.

Chapter Five: A Shortcut To Earning Big Money

Establishing income generation in your life is exactly what this book is about. I want to share how you can use property to earn the money you want to earn, so that you can get to where you need to be in life. It applies if you are looking to put together a property empire that will grow over time and create a legacy for your family and those who come after you. It applies if you are all about the cash, and you want to generate money now that you can spend and use to lift your standard of living to where you want it to be. Either way, this book is for you and will help you to understand how to make it happen.

I will show you how you can take the very simple steps I took to generate more income than you are likely to produce from any second job you will find.

In the second half of the book I will share with you some 'ninja cash-flow' strategies that I learned over time. I had to learn how to do it the hard way, on my own and by trial and error but I will share the successes so that you can copy them, and the nightmares so that you can avoid them.

I want you to take the fast track. This book is all about the money.

Chapter Six: Why Listen To Me?

Just so you are aware that I have actually been through this process myself I want to give you a brief snap-shot of where I am today. I do this not through a desire to show off, nor with a sense of false modesty. If you are going to read this book and be guided by me then you need to know that I know what I am talking about. You need to know that I actually walked the walk. Why would you listen to me if you didn't know that I had something sensible to say?

Here are the high level numbers. I own, co-own or jointly own three property portfolios with a combined equity of something over £2.3 million. I also have a deal packaging business, which is a very niche way of flipping houses. Within this business I have packaged in excess of 250 deals now. My deal packaging business, which secures properties and flips them on to investors without my having to put down any money at all, turns over in excess of 6 figures a year on a regular basis.

Please remember that all of this is only a part-time vocation for me. I am not someone who wants to work 80 hours a week. I really don't want to be one of those people who spend their lives sitting in an office looking out of a window watching life go by on the outside. I don't want to spend 40 years of my life working indoors, away from the light and fresh air so that I can then spend the time I have left trying to enjoy myself, possibly when I might be too old and decrepit to do the things that I really want to do. Such bucket-list pursuits may at some point include swimming in the Pacific, hang-gliding down Kilimanjaro, learning the joys of playing the Peruvian nose-flute from a Peruvian nose-flute player in the Peruvian Andes, or any number of other things.

You should take comfort from the fact that the ideas and practices that I am going to share with you are not new. Thousands of people have gone before you. Thousands of people have learned and implemented the very simple things that I am going to share with you in this book. Maybe I will present a slightly different approach? Hopefully I will inspire you and galvanise you into activity, because some activity is vital for success. The purpose of this book is to get you to start on your way and to show you how to become wealthy in the shortest time possible.

I first became involved in property in 1977. In that year, the year of Queen Elizabeth's Silver Jubilee, I bought my first property. It was a commercial building, and comprised a shop with rooms above it. I wasn't interested in the rooms above at the time because I was a retailer and merely wanted the shop.

I have to admit that I failed as a retailer. However, it took me approximately 30 years to fail and at the peak of my retail business we had 20 retail units operating. The recession of 1991-1992 was a major problem for us. We lost 50% of our turnover in 18 months. That is very hard to manage because your fixed costs – rent, business rates, staff and so-on remain just that; fixed.

We had no choice but to stop.

Although the retail trading company ceased to operate, by this time we also had a property company running alongside it. The property company had purchased some, but by no means all, of the shop units that we traded from when they were offered to us. The property company in turn leased the shop units to our trading company. The property arm of our business was mostly unaffected by the catastrophic events of 1991-1992, other than to the extent that it lost all its tenants on one day and had to find new ones quickly in order to keep paying the mortgages. It did find those new tenants and to my surprise, with unexpected ease and speed. Even in the recession of 1992 there were no shortage of businesses looking for trading premises.

When we made the decision to market the buildings for rental for the very first time to third parties, we did it slightly differently. We looked at the buildings and wondered what their potential might be. In those days there were no property education communities nor any property network meetings where you could share your ideas and learn from others, and so we did what seemed the obvious thing; we spoke to friends, and this is what we learned from them.

You'll recall that there were empty rooms above the retail spaces? Well they were present in each of the buildings but when we started to re-rent the buildings we didn't include the upper rooms in the rental agreements with the new retailers. Instead, we held them back to use ourselves. In 1997, only 20 years after the first purchase, we started to convert all the empty rooms over the shops into flats.

I was doing commercial conversions! I didn't even know at the time that I was doing commercial conversions but the result was that we developed eight flats and kept them to rent out. We still have them today and they are still rented out. The shops are also still rented out. Those buildings are the assets that underpin my virtually passive income lifestyle today.

The loans with which we purchased the buildings have long been paid off by the rent paid by the tenants who have occupied them over the years. Now the amount of money that comes in is such that all of my domestic bills, the payments which I have to make to maintain my standard of living, are paid by those rents received. That is my definition of financial freedom; to know that when you get out of bed in the morning, before you do anything at all, that all the bills that need paying to sustain your lifestyle are paid without having to do anything.

So let us get you on your way. I have written this book especially for you. Once you get started in property you will start to earn money, but it's not just about the money; it's what the money can do for you. Money gives you time and choice. It gives you the time to do what you want to do, when you want to do it and with the people that you want to do it with.

We need to get you to make changes in your life that thousands of others have made in their lives before you. In doing so, you can have the choice to stop doing what you are doing now, if that is what you want. You don't have to live the way you are living today.

- If you lay in bed at night dreading the time the alarm clock will go off, then this book is for you.

- If the daily commute to work is eating away at your soul, then this book is for you.

- If you would have enjoyed taking the kids to school instead of sitting in the traffic or on a train packed with commuters, then this book is for you.

- If you are fed up with being overlooked, overworked, undervalued and underpaid, then this book is for you.

- If you would have enjoyed the freedom to spend today working whilst wearing only your leopard-print onesie and flip-flops, then this book is for you.

- If you want the freedom to work when you want and to be able to say "flip it, let's head down the pub for a couple of hours' lunch", then this book is for you.

- If you want the freedom to spend time building a business and a legacy for your kids and grandkids with your life partner, instead of having to spend more time with your work colleagues than the one you love, then this book is for you.

- If you want to live somewhere else where the sun shines and it is warm every day, whilst still getting paid, then this book is for you.

- If you want the freedom to travel while the money is still coming in from your property investments, then this book is for you.

- If you want to do something that you love every day and reap rewards that you might not think possible today as you are reading this, then this book is for you.

I am honoured to be your guide and to show you what is possible.

Let's get started.

Chapter Seven: Flippin' Houses

I assume that by now you are ready to get started, or at least that you're ready to listen and to learn.

What are you going to hear? I am going to share with you the fundamentals of property investing so that you can start today, from scratch, in building a property portfolio to rent and which will bring you a virtually passive income from Day One. It will bring you capital growth that will build over time. I am also going to share with you one of the most powerful strategies in property, so you can make big chunks of cash virtually from Day One; that is the power of flipping houses. Buying and keeping houses is one of the most powerful ways to accumulate wealth over time. Flipping houses is one of the best ways in property to earn big chunks of cash.

The exciting thing is anyone can do it. If you do what I tell you to do, then you'll be able to do it too. You can keep houses to grow your wealth over time, or you can flip them to generate extra cash. You can then use that extra cash either to spend on your lifestyle so that you can live the life you want to live, or you can use it to build a "deposit war chest". What do I mean by this? I mean that you can save the money and build yourself a surplus of funds that can be used to buy more properties, more quickly. In that way your passive income grows month-on-month from the rental income, and over time you will experience the power of inflation and capital growth in your asset. Through these effects and the income that they generate, you can change your life.

YOUR FIRST INVESTMENT PROPERTY

How Do You Start?

Whether you are buying to hold the property, or you are buying to flip to generate cash, then the first thing you need to do is figure out the area you are going to work in; research is key. It doesn't matter where you live and you can buy properties anywhere. You need to know and understand the micro areas within your area that will work for investing and flipping. I am going to give you the short-cuts, hacks and power plays that hardnosed property professionals use to get an edge in this business.

If you are brand new to property and you don't have a clue where to start, then this is for you. I'm also going to share with you how not to do it – and this is how I did it at the beginning. Then I will tell you exactly what you should do so that you don't make the same mistakes I did. Let's get into the detail.

What I Did Wrong

When we first went to Manchester we didn't really have a clue where to buy, nor how to find out where to buy. We just rushed around, two "soft southerners" who had headed North to make their fortune on the somewhat grimy streets of Manchester. It was rumoured that if you looked very closely, some of those grimy streets might be paved with gold.

We did viewings all over our patch, we looked carefully at where we should buy and we tried to pinpoint the best area for us.

One critical factor was that it had to be in that area between the "Bronx", and the good areas that were slightly less affordable. We considered long and hard, evaluated the data and made a decision. Unfortunately, we got it wrong.

It was just inexperience that put us in the wrong place. As I completed my very first purchase I decided to visit a local letting agent to instruct them to find a tenant.

"I want working people. I want a property owning guarantor and I don't want tenants who are on housing benefits."

I was a southern landlord who had been in the rental game for many years. That's how it works in the South of England. I was set to be disappointed.

"No... I don't think we can get you any tenants who will meet those criteria."

"Why not? That is always my criteria!"

"Well you have bought in an area that is heavily dependent on Housing Benefit tenants. Not everyone works there. Even if they do work then it will probably be only part time and they will need housing benefit to pay their rent. As far as guarantors are concerned then you will struggle. These are very close knit communities. Anyone they know will probably not be acceptable as a guarantor."

I was devastated. I had got it all wrong. A very important lesson was learned, that being that when you're planning your next purchase or in my case, your first purchase, go and speak to the local letting agents first. They are the ones with the experience. They know where the hot-spots are and where the black-spots are. Indeed, I would go as far as to say that if you are just starting out then the only research you need to do on area is to go and visit all the letting agents in your town and ask them where you should buy.

Ask them where are the areas that they can let properties with minimal voids and no tenant issues. They will tell you because they have probably been on the patch for years. They know better than anyone and of course, they want an easy life. They want to work with a tenant profile that will cause them the minimum of issues. Listen to what they say and it will save you money.

Of course, that is not what I did. I went to them way too late in the process when I had already committed to buying a house. It was an error and one that I share with you now so that you can learn from my mistakes.

Chapter Eight: So W̶ Should You Buy?

If you study property online or in many other ͵ then you might end up feeling more confused t than you were at the beginning. I am going to simple, do it now strategies that anyone can use ͵ ͷ ͺmine area today. You should know that these are tried ͺ ͼested and I have used them myself. They work, and they are very simple. They have to be very simple because that is how I have to do things.

Let's not complicate this, Let's just make some money.

Hack Number 1 - Go And Visit Every Lettings Agent In Your Town

I'm not referring to the sales estate agents; I mean the letting agents. I also mean that you should make a physical visit not send an email or make a phone call. On this occasion you need to make the time to go in and look them in the eyes. If you phone or email you will just get ignored or fobbed off and will be unlikely to get the vital information that you need. Face-to-face, you can ask them for their help, tell them your plans, tell them that you want to build your own portfolio and that you are going to fund it in part by flipping other properties for profit. Ask them where you should buy as they know where you should buy. They know because they are out in the field every day. Unlike estate agents who just sell houses, letting agents have the responsibility to run properties for investors. They know that you have to buy in areas where you can find sensible tenants who will respect the property and pay the rent. They know the postcodes where you will find the most sensible tenants. They know the actual streets where you should buy. They will tell you which end of the street that you should buy in. If you tell them that you want them to let the properties that you will be buying and flipping, then it's in their interests to give you the because it will ultimately make their life easier. Everyone wants an easy life at work. Letting agents are exactly the same.

is is very important information to obtain; the information will help to keep you away from the "Bronx". There is a Bronx type area in every town and you should not buy property there. One definition of the Bronx is an area where, if the tenants leave a rented property either during the rental term or at the end of the tenancy, then they're likely to take the boiler and the copper piping with them. That is not where you should buy even if prices are lower there.

How do you know if you are in the "Bronx"? Well there are tell-tale signs to look out for. Watch out for sofas abandoned in the street (yes, that is what I meant). The first time I came across this phenomenon I didn't understand the full implications of it. I was being taken to view several houses by a sales estate agent. He was driving us around in his car and every time we turned a corner we came upon an abandoned sofa. We had seen several by now and I had to ask him why they were there.

He explained, "Well it was a lovely sunny weekend and of course, because all of these houses are Victorian terraces then they don't really have gardens. When it's warm and sunny the residents want to be outside. They don't have garden furniture so they push their sofas into the street. It's great while they enjoy the sun but inevitably they will also enjoy a few drinks while they are out. Then they totter off to bed a bit worse for wear leaving the sofas behind. Overnight it rained. The sofas got soaked and now they can't put them back in the house again. It happens quite often."

This is a sign that you are in the Bronx. Do not buy in the Bronx.

Don't forget to visit all the letting agents in your town and keep very careful notes on what they tell you. By the end of several visits you should have a detailed breakdown of the areas in your town, where to buy and where not to buy. This information is priceless but we are only at the beginning of our research into where we should buy for investing and flipping.

Hack Number 2 – Have A Look At The Major Supermarkets In Your Town

Supermarkets became more prolific in the 1990's and in particular following the turn of the 21st century. All the big players opened stores at a rapid pace. Supermarkets are run by very clever people, and they pay huge sums to research an area before they spend even greater amounts of money actually committing to an area and opening a new store. We haven't got that sort of budget and they aren't going to share their data with us, but there is a way that we might be able to get a flavour of what they have found to help us on our way.

Before I go on, I have to qualify what I say about supermarkets generally because not all of them will help our research and for different reasons. City centre stores are no help at all because they don't tell us what we need to know. They serve the city centre. Similarly, out of town stores in purpose built locations where several different stores are located all together but isolated and away from the town and with huge car parks, can be discounted too. They will not tell us what we need to know.

What we are looking for are stores that are built in urban areas and stores that might serve the lower demographic groups as the majority of their customer base. What we are looking for are the areas where good honest working people live and bring up their families. These are our primary target areas to find below market value deals ("BMV" as it's referred to in the trade) or discounts to the market value. The people who will usually sell you your deals will predominately live in streets made up of Victorian terraced properties, but they may also live in tidy cul-de-sacs made up of semi-detached three bedroomed houses built later in the 20th century. They will drive relatively new cars but not necessarily prestigious German marques and their young children will play ball games outside the house or on the lawn (if it's a semi) with their pals at weekends. You get the picture; where these people live is where your best deals are going to be found.

Supermarkets target these demographics as customers for their stores; if you can find out where these people live then you will have found out, in general terms as part of your research, where you should target your focus to find your deals.

Let's consider and then locate the stores that serve these people. If we can find the stores that serve them specifically then we will know that they live close by. Hopefully that makes sense; let's keep going.

You have all been in one of these types of stores. The giveaway is the way they are laid out by the store merchandisers. You can recognise the stores at the entrance. As soon as you walk in what is the first thing you will see? Probably they will have reduced seasonal items, barbecue stuff and beer in the summer, and reduced barbecue stuff and beer in the winter. Walk past this and what do you see then? If it is two to three aisles of clothing, then you are in the right place. For our purposes this is a BMV store. Keep moving through the store. What do you see then? If the next couple of aisles contain fruit and vegetables but, in truth, the displays are less than eye catching and some of the produce looks a bit apologetic for being there, then you are definitely in the right place. As you move further into the store if there appears to be a disproportionately large offering of frozen foods then that's also a sign you are in the right place. This isn't an exact science but you will get an impression of the store as you move through and you will know if you are in the right place.

There are some stores that do not help us in this research and you should discount them for the purposes of your research. By all means though, go and do some shopping in them because all the stores I am about to mention are great stores.

Waitrose stores are great stores but unfortunately are of little assistance to us in our quest for houses we might be able to flip. That is because their customer profile is very specific and they tend to site their stores in upmarket areas. That is why they don't merchandise their stores as indicated above. Upmarket areas are great places to buy, hold and flip houses but the cost of buying houses in these areas may be too high if you are just starting out. By all means let's work our way up to these types of properties but in the beginning let's wait and try somewhere else.

Similarly, Morrison's stores don't help our research either. This is because all Morrison's stores appear to be merchandised in the same way wherever they are sited. The first thing you see when you go into a Morrison's store is their "Market Place" set out beautifully with fruit and vegetables. It gives no clue to what the store demographic is.

You have to be a bit careful with Aldi and Lidl also. The early stores they opened were very helpful. They knew who their customer was at the time and they located the stores in areas where our customers live today. However, in the credit-crunch era of 2008 onwards things changed a little bit. Wealthier people discovered that they too could save money in these stores. They realised that cheaper fruit and veg could taste just as good even if it was a slightly weird shape. Aldi and Lidl rose to the challenge. They opened new stores and grew their businesses rapidly. The difficulty for us is that the newer stores are all very smart and are located in all different types of areas. Be careful when adding Aldi and Lidl stores to your research. You need to look at the older stores only.

By far the most helpful stores to our research in this area are Tesco and Asda. They have many types of store and work with all types of demographic as customers. If you look carefully though, you will find stores with the type of layout outlined above and they will be the stores that serve our target customer. Another word of warning; sometimes you will find the store but it doesn't appear to be in one of our target areas. Why would this be? Well quite simply, it is because a Tesco or Asda store has to be of a certain size to work as a store. They want to site the store in a certain area but if there isn't a suitable place for it to go or planning issues might be to troublesome, long and drawn out, they may choose to open the store somewhere else. Chance are they won't be too far away from their ideal location, but they won't be on the doorstep of their target customer. Their problem now is to get the target customer into the store. This is the solution and it's a stroke of genius.

The answer is the free bus. Both firms run a free bus in certain locations and it's a key resource for us. The free bus comes out of the store, drives to the place where the chosen demographic chooses to live and then drives up and down the streets where its customers are based, letting them on and letting them off. It then drives back to the store only to repeat the process over again throughout the day. Both Asda and Tesco know where their customers live. They have the same customers that we do. To complete your research in these areas all you actually have to do is get on to the free Asda or Tesco bus and see where it goes. It will take you to your customers.

So we've done our research, it has cost us nothing to this point which is really good and we are ready to start doing some viewings. We now know where to look, and we have to decide what we are going to look at.

Chapter Nine: What To Buy?

For anyone starting out on this adventure to build a property portfolio and to fund it, or to enhance their lifestyle by flipping properties then I would definitely begin by looking at houses and not flats. Houses are the way forward.

Why should beginners not work with flats? Well there are several reasons. When I was a beginner, I bought a few flats and it proved to be a mistake. The purpose of this book is to help you get off to a great, money making start on your property investing journey. Don't make the mistakes I made. Don't buy flats until you know what you are doing.

In England most flats you will come across will be leasehold. The mysteries of leasehold are to be expanded upon in another book at another time, but the bottom line for you is that working in leasehold flats will make your life harder. Owning the lease of a flat is not the same as owning the freehold. Someone else will own the freehold and you will be their tenant. Your rights with respect to the flat will be laid down in the lease. You will be required to pay a Ground Rent which will typically be in the region of £125 every year. You must not break the terms of the lease and in practice this can mean that the scope to add value will be very limited. If you are in a block of flats you will not be able to start turning a one bed flat into a two bed flat without the landlord's consent, which they may or may not give. You cannot start putting in extra windows and making other structural alterations without the landlord's consent either, and in my experience you probably won't get consent.

Then there is the consideration of mortgages. Will you get a mortgage at the level you need it and if you are going to flip it will the ultimate purchaser be able to get a mortgage? Both these factors can be influenced by the term of the lease which is key here. Lenders are now very cautious about the number of years that remain on a flat's lease. It's common for a new-build flat to have a term of 99 years or commonly 125 years granted in the lease. The problem is that the years tick away. I bought a flat in 2008. The flat had an original term of 99 years but it had been sold as new to the original owner in 1988. So when I bought it still had 79 years left on the lease, long enough to see me out and if I was gone then I wouldn't really care anyway. At that time, mortgage companies had no issue with that length of unexpired term. As a rule of thumb if there were still going to be at least 40 years left on the lease at the expiry of the mortgage, then all would be well and they would lend. In simple terms, on the flat I bought in 2008 I wanted a 25-year mortgage on the property. At the end of that mortgage on this particular property then there would still be a lease of 54 years unexpired. No problem for the lender, all was good.

But things have changed. After the credit crunch of 2008, lenders got very nervous and changed criteria for loans on flats. In particular, lenders have changed the criteria they need to see with regard to the unexpired part of the lease. Nowadays, if you have a flat with any term less than 70 years unexpired from TODAY then that is a problem for mortgage lenders.

When did that happen? Why was I not consulted?

Those of you with a strong arithmetical bent will have grasped pretty quickly that my flat today, at the time of writing, has a term of only 69 years remaining. Suddenly, unexpectedly, this is a problem. I have had to go to the freeholder and ask for a lease extension. It depends on your freeholder as to whether they are likely to grant such an extension. There is a formal legal route that you, as a long lease tenant can go down to secure your lease extension. The rules are very clear and any long-lease tenant is entitled to an additional term of 90 years which is added to the unexpired term. Crucially once you go through this process then the Ground Rent is also reduced to that of a "peppercorn" – in effect zero.

However, the freeholder has rights too and is entitled to a payment of money to compensate them for the lease extension that they are forced by law to give. The negotiation is also very carefully laid out in the statute but in the real world it is not all that straightforward. In the real world, you feel obliged, as I did, to approach the freeholder informally to see if you can sort this out between you. Why would you not do that? You are a nice person and it is only the right thing to do out of courtesy to the other side. Sadly, the other side doesn't always extend the same courtesy back to you. Make no mistake, they usually know the rules. They know what you are entitled to and how it all works but they spend months delaying the process and making ridiculous demands that they know will not stand up in a tribunal if it got to that point. During the process you inevitably incur legal fees and usually have to instruct expert surveyors in the field of lease extensions.

This is an example that illustrates how these things can and do go. The freeholder is usually experienced and they know what they are likely to get. They also know that it will cost you around £3,000 to take the case to the tribunal and so they position their demands in such a way that they exceed the statutory rights by about £3,000 in the hope and expectation that you will pay them the extra just to bring the matter to a conclusion. They know that by doing this, at least you will save yourself the stress and heartache of having to go to the tribunal. Not cool.

If it's not enough to have to deal with the freeholders and the lenders, then it's entirely possible that the other long leaseholders are an issue that might have to be dealt with also. What do I mean by that? What do you have to look out for?

Many newly built blocks of flats, especially in the North of England were built between 2003 and 2007. Whenever I have the opportunity to buy a flat, one of the first questions I ask is "When was it built?" The reason is this; in older blocks the long leaseholder profile was different. Generally, in the 1980's and 1990's these flats were sold to owner occupiers. People bought them as their home. They lived in them and took pride as owners. They created a pleasant, safe, calm environment. It was a pleasure to own in that kind of development. In the blocks built and sold between 2003 and 2008 that was not always the case. In my experience flats sold at that time were more commonly sold to investors off-plan and these investors sometimes lived elsewhere, maybe hundreds of miles away.

This would often lead to difficulties. In a block of say, 25 apartments you may have all of them come to the rental market at the same time. The investors would be competing against other investors to rent out their apartments first because they all had mortgage payments to make on a monthly basis so they needed the flats to be occupied and quickly. This led to a race to the bottom in terms of rents agreed. The shiny brochures on which the investors made the decision to buy, may have promised rents in the region of £675 per calendar month but it soon became clear that the real market rent was going to be £450 per calendar month. That alters things a bit. On top of this, we then have to consider management costs. If you buy a flat in a block, then you have to pay the management company fees to look after the common areas and maintain the building. This figure might start at a modest £50 a month or so but quite quickly could go up to £120 or £130 a month. I've seen those figures in my own experience.

The arithmetic is simple. An investor has bought into a development and owns a flat. The investor only gets around two thirds of the expected rent and in addition the maintenance costs eat into that reduced income. The mortgage still has to be paid. Then they might get a difficult tenant who doesn't pay the rent or who trashes the flat; remember, the quality of tenant has altered dramatically just in the process of filling the flats. The investor's income is now virtually non-existent and costs have gone up again. This is now becoming an unhappy investment for an unhappy investor.

Investors are people too. Things happen in their lives, circumstances change and who knows what challenges they may now be under? Their financial wellbeing might be affected and so, out of sight being out of mind, they decide to stop paying the management charges because they see it as a cost that they can get away with not paying in the face of their immediate struggle.

I have seen blocks where this has happened. The stress point is that not just a single investor/owner has stopped paying, but as many as half of the owners have stopped paying the maintenance charge. There is a critical point where the maintenance company can no longer maintain its service nor maintain the development. The development can then go into a self-inflicted decline and the quality of facilities and their maintenance is in a tail spin. It becomes even harder to attract decent tenants to live in the building. Rents fall again, the management company resigns and without a management company in place the flats cannot be mortgaged so the owners cannot sell.

What a mess!

This type of development is in a downwards spiral of decline. It can take years, and a huge commitment of energy by somebody, usually an alliance of the compliant owners to sort it all out. There are hundreds of developments like this all over the North of England. Sometimes students come to me asking my advice because they have found an opportunity to buy one of these flats and hope to buy it with the intention to flip and make a profit. Please do not buy one of these flats. You may not be able to raise finance on it anyway if that is how you intend to secure it, but even if you can, there is no resale value in the development at all. Typically, all the flats would have been sold within a few months of the construction of the building and then there will be no public record of any further transactions. Usually, none of the original owners has sold. This is because they all paid in the region of £120,000 and have mortgages in the region of £90,000 to service. The type of offers they are receiving for their flats would be in the region of £40-60,000. They cannot accept offers at that level as they will not be able to clear their mortgages and their deposit monies will be lost. Their only way out will be to find money from other sources to pay everything off and then they just have to walk away and put it down to experience.

For all these reasons then I hope you will heed my warning; if you are starting out, just buy houses.

Houses are freehold, there are no service charges and they don't have management companies. You can make the changes you want subject to the local planning department and building control at the council. Don't buy flats, buy houses instead; houses are the safer bet either for building your own portfolio or for flipping your way to more wealth.

Chapter Ten: What Are You Looking For? What Is A Deal?

How will you know what to buy? What are the basic criteria you need to look for in a potential purchase? We have decided that we are going to buy houses at the start, and let's assume that you have found a house that you like the look of. How do you know if it is a "deal"?

If you are just starting out, then there are basic numbers that you need to know.

For an investment purchase that you intend to keep, generally most industry professionals talk about "Gross Yield" when assessing whether a deal is great or not. My understanding of how to calculate gross yield is as follows:

You take the gross rent that you realistically believe you will receive over a 12-month period and you divide that figure by the total acquisition costs of the house. These costs will include the purchase price, any tax and transactional costs, solicitor's fees, and so-on, as well as any money you will spend to bring the property up to good lettable condition. Hopefully you will find a little gem that will need very little money spent on it, but beware this trip wire that I have seen so many friends stumble over.

I will use very round numbers to illustrate the point. Let's assume that the open market value of a house in good lettable condition is £100,000 and the house is in the North of England. I understand that if you live in London or the South East then this figure sounds fictional and unachievable, but if it helps you, just add a zero to the figures and hopefully the example will work for you. This is just a notional example, not a real house – stay with me.

So we have a £100,000 house but we can buy it for £80,000. On the face of it then this property is £20,000 below market value. This would be a great buy. We want to find them all like that. It would be a really great buy if all it needed was just a really good clean up and maybe some new flooring. There are properties like that and you will find them. However, this is not actually one of those.

When we look closely there are some significant upgrading works required before we can say that it is in good lettable condition. Electrics, heating, a bit of damp, gutters and downpipes, maybe windows and doors; there is work to do. By the time we have finished, it looks like we are going to spend around £20,000 in order to bring an £80,000 purchase up to standard. We will be spending £100,000 on a house that is worth £100,000.

This is not a deal! Do not do this deal!

I have seen new friends in the industry do this so many times. You have to have the value of the works required in your calculations when you are working out the gross yield. At the point when you are doing your calculations to decide whether the deal is a deal either to buy or to sell, you will not have these figures to hand, so how do you estimate what the upgrade costs will be? I have a whole chapter dedicated to this point later in the book. Even if you have no experience of doing this I will show you the way.

Gross Yield And Stacking The Deal

So you now have all the figures for your acquisition costs. Let us pause for a moment before you do the sum. You will recall that I said above that you take the total rental figure that you realistically believe you will receive as part of this calculation. I chose my words carefully. Will you receive 12 months' rent in every 12-month period? Will you receive all the rent in full or might there be arrears? Will a tenant leave and a new one move in? How will this affect your numbers? Will there be a void period between tenancies? How long will that be? In reality you will have no idea whether these things will happen and how your projections would be affected if they did. There is no definitive answer to these questions, but we have to pick a number to reflect the possibility. For this reason, I use eleven-months' gross rent as my estimate for what I will receive in the year. There is no science to that number; we have to decide on a number and that is what I do. If you are feeling more nervous about it then you might use ten-months' rent-roll as your number. That should be very safe in most reasonable circumstances.

To find the gross yield you divide the rent-roll figure you are using by the total cost of acquisition and express it as a percentage. If you can find a double digit percentage gross yield in an area that you have already identified through you research as being one of your goldmine areas, then it is likely to be a pretty good investment. See if you can find properties with gross yields of 9-11%. Those will work. For most of the UK today you are likely to find houses with gross yields of 7-8%. These may work also, but they may be more marginal so it is critical that you really do your numbers carefully on these. You don't want to "forget" anything and get a nasty surprise going forward. The cash-flow on that property should be sufficient to pay all of the running expenses of the house for years to come and still leave you with a profit. This deal "stacks".

What does "stack" mean? A deal has to stack for it to be profitable. It is a calculation just one stage further on from calculating the gross yield figure. To find out if a deal stacks, you are in effect doing a monthly mini profit and loss account on the property. This is worked out on a monthly basis. You take the gross monthly rent and subtract all of the monthly costs you will encounter to make sure it works. The typical reductions are letting agent fees, service charge and ground rent if it is a flat, insurance, the mortgage payment and Section 24 tax if you are buying in your personal name. Don't forget you also need to subtract a figure to represent voids, maintenance and arrears to get the true stack figure.

Let's assume you have done all the arithmetic and have worked out, using pessimistic assumptions, that on a monthly basis this particular house will rent and at the end of each month you will be left with a profit after all costs. What does that profit have to be, in order to be regarded as a good deal?

I believe that in the industry generally it is regarded that if a Buy-to-Let property stacks, and the profit is a minimum of £250 per month wherever you are in the UK, then that is considered a good deal. Of course, you can look for deals that stack at a higher level and you may well find them, but I am trying to keep you safe. I am trying to let you know what the minimums are that you need to make your new property portfolio work. We can get more advanced as we move forward in our property journey and we can introduce more cutting-edge ways to add cash-flow to our property assets as we grow.

For now, let's just get started and make some money.

Once you know that you have a great deal you can safely buy it and put it into your portfolio and wait. It will never hurt you. Those are the type of properties you should hold.

Chapter Eleven: Should You Buy In The North Or The South? A Perspective Based On Experience Of Both

The example discussed in the previous chapter was pretty clear cut. Let's now muddy the waters a bit. If you are based in the South of England, then you will not be able to find many houses for £100,000 and the cost of entry into the market will be much higher. However, what we find is that the rent achievable on the property will not be proportionately higher. With a slightly higher rent-roll and a very much higher purchase cost then we can see very quickly what will happen to the gross yield. It will be much lower. Gross yields of 3% or 4% are not uncommon today in great swathes of London and the South East. That means that when you come to stack the deal you may find that there is very little positive cash-flow in the property. Indeed, there may even be a negative cash-flow.

Does this rule this property out as an investment? Well, I am going to say "not necessarily". This is the part where you have to be brave and have a bit of a crystal-ball. Let's assume you have worked out your gross yield on the Southern property and you've had a look to see if it stacks. The answer is that in the real world it might not. What do you do? Do you just walk away? Do you say that only properties north of Milton Keynes now work as investment properties?

I don't believe that to be true and in fact, I know that property deals are done in London and the South East of England every day. We need to look more closely at property investment as a whole.

Of course yield is important, and I know that buying only with reference to yield will keep you safe, but it may also rob you over time. What generates wealth in property over time is not just the yield, or the cash-flow from the house, but the total return.

Let me illustrate the point. In 2006-7 I purchased two very different properties. One was in the South of England and one was in the North of England. The purchases were within 6 months of each other. The purchase price for each was very close to £75,000. The cash-flow from each was, and remains in the region of £250 pcm. Today, in 2019, the property in the South of England is worth in the region of £145,000. The property in the North of England is worth... £75,000.

And so the question here is; "Is yield enough?"

Surely we should consider the potential of total return when we are making our investments?

We have to consider not only the income we will receive, but also the possibility of capital growth over time when we buy a property. The issue with this is that the naysayers will say that you should not factor in the potential of capital growth over time because it is not guaranteed. They will say that this is the property equivalent of crystal-ball gazing. To the extent that capital growth is not guaranteed then the naysayers are correct, but sometimes in life you have to take a calculated assessment of what may happen going forward. I have struggled with this over many years of my life in property. I made decisions based on the accepted wisdom of buying property based on yield and although it may have kept me safe from the downside, it has also cost me very dearly by limiting my exposure to the upside. I have made mistakes which have cost me huge amounts of money. I am going to share this with you now so you can avoid the mistakes I've made.

In 2004 I decided to go North to buy property. The reason that I went was that at that time, property prices in the South seemed unaffordable. Relatively, prices in the South back then were very similar to prices in the South today – very high. I believed that houses in the South of England were unaffordable and my money wouldn't go far in the South since I needed large deposits. Maybe I could raise one or two deposits but then

I would run out. If I put all my money into one property in the South and then I found a difficult tenant who didn't pay me then I would be looking at significant losses on a monthly basis from which I would never recover. It might over time even threaten the viability of the purchase and it might stop me building my property portfolio.

I thought that if I went to the North of England I would be able to buy property more cheaply meaning that my deposits would go further. Other advantages would be that the cost of entry in the North was much lower. I would be able to spread my risk by buying multiple properties and get my rent from multiple tenants. It was extremely unlikely that all of my tenants would stop paying their rent at the same time so this spread would help me. I would be able to leverage multiple deposits and get mortgages more easily, and because the gross yield was relatively higher, the purchases would be more secure since the income from the houses would leave a tidy profit at the end of the month to cover all eventualities.

This was logical thinking in so far as it went. The fact that I hadn't considered in my calculations was the effect of capital growth over time. The bottom line is that in the North of England, in the housing stock that I bought over the period from 2004 to 2019, I have had virtually no capital growth at all.

Between us, my business partner and myself purchased over 50 properties in the period 2004 to 2008. The pattern of growth went something like this. During the period 2004 to 2007 we experienced significant capital growth, but then in 2008 the credit crunch led to a property market crash and prices fell back to levels last seen in 2003. Let me give this some perspective; from 2003 we had been buying houses initially at prices around £35-£40,000. These houses were in decent letting areas. In the period from 2004 to 2007 the prices of these houses rose so that in 2007 we were paying close to £80,000 for the same houses. Prices continued to rise. We actually believed that they would reach 6 figures and we would be wealthy as a result. Indeed, the last house I agreed to purchase, just before the crash really kicked in, was at a price of £101,000. This was a two bed terraced house in Leigh village near Saddleworth in Greater Manchester. I agreed this purchase at a critical time. The downturn had begun and lenders were starting to pull out of the market. As the market turned, it became clear that I had offered too much and that I was going to pay six figures for an asset that was dropping in value as I watched the evening news on a daily basis. I pulled out and I know that the house was subsequently sold at £94,000 quite shortly afterward.

From 2003-2008 there was significant capital growth. In the crash of 2008, prices fell back to around the £40,000 level again and they stayed there for some years. Only now as I write this in 2019 have prices returned to something like 2007 levels. That is over ten years with no capital growth whatsoever.

Now what if, instead of buying over 50 houses in the north-west of England, we had bought just five houses in the south-east of England. Those five houses over the last ten years would have enjoyed significant capital growth. Those five houses would have more than doubled in value. What if I had bought those five houses in and around London? Those houses would also have more than doubled in value. The purchase of those five properties alone would have made me wealthy.

The challenge would have been to support the cost of running the houses over the 10-year period, since the rent wouldn't have been enough to support all the costs of running the house. Those deals would not have stacked and the houses wouldn't even have cash-flowed. We would have had to put our hands in our pockets every month to pay the shortfall.

Do you want yield, or are you more interested in total return? How do you factor in the potential growth in the house over a period of years when you are doing your calculations? Should you factor in capital growth to your calculations when you are planning to buy a house?

If you are buying to hold, then you need capital growth over time; you need asset inflation. Asset inflation makes heroes out of all of us.

I will make my view very clear on this, and I'll state that my opinion has changed as I have got older and lived through several property cycles. The bottom line is that if you are buying to hold, if you are buying to build wealth and create a legacy then you have to buy for capital growth. Cash-flow alone will not make you wealthy. Even in the North of England, where potentially you can get houses with a double digit gross yield after all expenses, you are still only going to net around £200 per month per property. You can build a useful amount of cash-flow on a monthly basis but it will never produce life changing wealth. In order to achieve that you have to invest in the South of England.

So why don't we establish a plan like this? If you live in the North of England, then start your property adventure by flipping properties on your doorstep. By the time you have completed your first five flips then you will have learned how to do it properly and you will have built a significant amount of money so that you now have a really healthy sized deposit to buy wherever you wish in the UK. Take the money and invest in a house in the South of England. This one is to keep. This one is for you to put away and forget about. This one, over time will grow in value and make you wealthy. While you are waiting for your wealth to grow you can head North again, do several more flips and build another pot of money so you can then head South and buy again. This is a plan. This will work.

What if you live in the South? Well you could head North, where money does go further and start sourcing the first of your flip projects there. You can try to put together a team locally who might deal with the project on a day-to-day basis. The thing is, it's always harder to manage these schemes if you are geographically some distance away and are trying to do this remotely. I think your best way forward might be to look for your projects in the South, near to where you live. Yes, the cost of entry will be higher. Yes, the cost of the refurbishment might be higher. However, you will have the advantage of control over the project as it will be on your doorstep. Of course, at the end of the refurbishment, the profit per flip will be much higher.

Squaring The Circle

The question then comes up, as to how you are going to fund the purchase of these investments? The answer is very simple. You have to learn the process of flipping houses.

For every house that you buy to keep in your investment pot forever, the ones that will bubble away and grow and will make you wealthy over time, then you have to aim to buy two houses with the intention from the start of making them into projects that you're going to add value to, so that you can sell them again onto the open market at a profit. The profit from those flips is where the cash comes from to grow your business. You've got to learn how to flip. The profit that you make from your flips will not only sustain you in your property adventure while your investment properties are starting to grow, but will provide the funds to buy your first or second investment properties as you move forward.

Remember that you don't need many houses to become wealthy, as long as you buy them in the right places. Over the next 10 years they could grow in value and completely change your financial situation. I have a pal who bought six properties in and around Essex from 2013 onwards. He bought them on mortgages and, yes, he has used his education to help him introduce more advanced strategies with respect to tenanting the properties to cover the costs as he has gone along. He recently had them revalued and they have doubled in value in the last 6 years. The increase in the value of these houses has made him wealthy – in just 6 years.

Here is the point; it is not too late to get into property. It is not just the people who bought property 30 years ago that can become wealthy as a result of it. You need to start today. If you start today property will transform your financial life and I say that with full volition. I believe it. The reason I believe it is that I've seen it happen. Over and over again, friends have gone into property at different times during the last 30-40 years while I have been active in property and have made money. The only reservation I will state right now, that you need to heed, is that you have to know what you're doing. If you follow my systems, if you follow my advice you will know what you're doing.

The first project that you should take on should be a flip. That first flip project, properly executed will set you on your way. You should earn no less than £20,000 on your first flip no matter where you are in the UK. If you follow my systems, then you will earn at least that on every flip. Maybe the first five projects that you do will be flips. Because once you learn how to do it properly, it becomes a habit. You really enjoy the process because you've learned where all the pitfalls are, and you've put your team together that can deliver the projects. After five flips you will have at least £100,000 in the bank and will be ready to go for your future property investments. By this time, you know how to make money from flipping houses. You get the buzz. It is like a drug. You will not stop doing it. You cannot stop doing it. I'm going to have to remind you to take the money you will be earning so that you can buy an investment property which you will keep to build your wealth in later years.

We have a plan. This is exciting. We are on our way.

Of course you have to fund that first flip. I know that. And you might be sitting reading this thinking that you do not have any money and do not know where to begin, but I am going to help you there too. I have a whole section on funding later in this book, and that will get you on your way.

But let's do one thing at a time...

Chapter Twelve: Putting Your Power Team Together

Now that we know *where* we are going to buy and what we are going to buy, we need to start thinking about the process itself and how we are going to move forward with a purchase, either to flip or to keep.

These are the people you need in your property life, what I term your *Power Team*. You will need the following:

A favourite estate agent who understands what you want, and who is prepared to work with you to help you get it. They will be only too happy if you turn up knowing what you want and how you are going to pay for it. This makes you a real prospect for them; don't forget they are there to sell houses after all.

An accountant who understands property. This is absolutely vital. The climate is changing fast in the property world. There is no doubt that over the last few years the government has introduced a series of tax changes in the property world which, on the face of them, will make it costlier for property professionals to operate. The changes to stamp duty, capital gains tax, the treatment of mortgage interest relief, and so much more has meant that we have all had to become much more professional in the conduct, not only of our property business but also of our tax affairs. My personal view is that the assault (and I thought carefully about using that word before I wrote it down) on the property industry by those in power has been unparalleled. I cannot remember any other time during my business life when any particular section of the economy has been subjected to such a relentless attack by the powers that be, as that which the property business has been subjected to in the last few years.

That doesn't mean that you should be frightened off. What you need to do is to be more professional in your approach. If you are starting out in your property journey today (presumably which is why you are reading this book), then if you get the correct advice from the outset, you can mitigate or avoid so much of the regulation that has been put in place. The secret is in getting clued up before you start so that your structure is sound, and that you future-proof yourself against any future changes.

Anyway, back to the membership of your power team.

A mortgage broker who knows their stuff. You want one who is active, busy and who is up to date with, and has access to the full market.

A solicitor who is an active property based solicitor. If you can find one who is a property investor themselves that would be a preferable and a great help to your cause. There are certain criteria that I look for when choosing a solicitor. The most important thing is that you can contact them and that they will respond to you. I think we've all had experience of solicitors who you can never get hold of on the phone, and who never call you back. That is a complete no-no for me. The solicitors I use always call me back. Of course I don't expect to pick up the phone to call them and for them to answer straight away. I understand that they have other clients and I understand that they have their own deadlines and pressures. That said, I do expect them to call me back at the earliest opportunity; the next day at the latest. I hear nightmare stories of messages just going into a black hole and of solicitors who do not respond. That is disrespectful and bad for our property business.

Find yourself an active property solicitor.

You're probably wondering where you can find these people? The easiest way in my view is to go into the property forums on Facebook and just ask. We are very fortunate today that there is such a readily accessible public resource which is available to us with just a couple of clicks from our smartphones. This very day, as I am writing this paragraph, I have noted that a friend of mine went online and asked in a property forum who might recommend a great Buy-to-Let mortgage broker. Within a few minutes there were over a dozen recommendations, all of them very professional and great at what they do. What a fantastic resource to have at our disposal; it was not always like that.

When I started out property was a bit of a lonely game. I worked on my own and I had no-one to bounce ideas off or to ask for advice. The biggest turning point in my property business has been discovering groups of likeminded people who have walked the ground before me and who are so open in offering advice and support. It is all freely available too! If you don't have one already then I suggest you set up your Facebook profile and get yourself out there. Have a look at some of the property forums and join a few of them. Have a look at the interactions within the group and decide if you want to stay. When you leave a couple, join a couple more. In the space of a month or so you will have found the communities that you like, and you will have access to thousands of people who will help and support you. There are sometimes over 20,000 people in these communities from which you will get a lot of support. My favourite property forum is the Progressive Property Investors Community. It is a very constructive community that will always have a suggestion or advice to help you move forwards. Give it a try.

Aside from online property communities, there is of course the route of getting personal recommendations. I would suggest that you be a little bit careful when it comes to these. People will tell you that they have a mortgage broker and that their mortgage broker is the best mortgage broker in the entire world. Maybe they are recommending someone who did a great job for them when they were buying their house, their family home. That is not the same as a broker who is working with property professionals on a daily basis. You need to find one of these to complete your power team.

Chapter Thirteen: Builders

This is absolutely key to your success. You are going to need a network of excellent building contractors if you are going to buy properties that are a little bit tired and unloved, and then bring them up to standard to keep and rent out, or to flip for a profit.

You may well be tempted to do the work yourself and it would be very tempting for the first time investor or flipper to roll their sleeves up and dive in themselves. There are two schools of thought about this and I have followed both in the past. The first school would say that when you are starting out then you need to save as much money as possible and so you should do all the work yourself. That demands fitting the renovations and repairs in around everything else that is going on in your life. It means spending the day at work (because you will still be in your job at this time) and then coming home, grabbing a bite to eat and spending your evenings doing DIY tasks around your investment property. Then you fall into bed, grab your 6-7 hours sleep and get up to repeat the whole process the following day. When the weekends come around, again you can spend the whole of the weekend every weekend until the project is finished, rubbing down, re-plastering walls, updating bathroom suites, painting ceilings and so-on. Do not try to do any work on electrics or gas as you most certainly need professionals for these tasks.

The problem with this plan is that the grind of it will wear you down. I know; I have tried it. It always talks six times longer than you planned and, if I am honest, the results are usually nowhere near good enough. If you are going to add value to a house to flip it, then the finish has to be good. You will not get your target price out of the house if you don't get a good enough finish with your renovations. For this reason, I am going to suggest that you take a different approach and recruit local contractors to help you.

Will this be more expensive? Well it depends on how you view the task.

The big bonus for me is that you get your life back. You can rest in the evenings and stay fresh for work. You will see your family which is a very important reason why you are doing this in the first place. Your weekends become your own again too.

Of course this approach has its own problems too. You have to become a project manager which means making sure that the right people are on site when they are needed. You have to find them in the first place and you have to make sure they turn up. You have to get them to quote for work and you have to approve their quotes. On the face of it, you might think that this approach is way more expensive than the DIY approach but in truth it can be far more cost effective. You save time and the work is usually done quicker. You can get the house back on the market and ready for sale weeks earlier than if you were doing all the work yourself.

The opportunity cost of DIY has to be factored in as well. If the house is finished quicker, then you can get it back on the market for sale quicker. While you are waiting for the house to sell so you can get your profit, you can be looking for your next project. As soon as the money comes in for one you can get started on the next one.

The key to success in flipping a house for profit, is speed. As a project manager, if you follow my advice and take that strategy towards the renovation work then you have to be hands-on with the contractors. This is far preferable to being hands-on with the work yourself, and having to work away into the early hours of the morning trying to get the job done yourself.

There is a halfway-house of course. Maybe you are a builder? You might be a carpenter, a plasterer, or someone who has been working on building sites for years? If this is the case for you, then because of your work, you may have the skills to complete the task on a professional level. You may have access to pals, or family members who also have the skills that you might not have yourself, but that you need to finish the job. One of my pals is a carpenter, and this is what he does in relation to his properties. He works with other contractors all the time who have the skills to help him finish his refurbishments.

Maybe you have family who have the necessary skills? Leverage their time and experience. They can help you make money.

What if you don't know anyone who can help you with the project? Here are a couple of must-try hacks and ninja-strategies to help you get to the right people, that can help you make money.

First there are the more obvious places to start. I suggest you try Check-a-Trade or other similar resources and that you go through and look at the reviews for tradesmen on there. Always pick a contractor with lots of reviews; if he is clearly busy and if he is getting great reviews then you need him on your team. I found a fantastic plumbing and heating engineer just by doing that. It might be obvious but it works. Yes, you might have to kiss a few frogs along the way, but at the end of the day you will find your prince (or princess)!

Next, go along to your local BNI breakfast networking group. BNI is a national organisation and was set up for anyone in business to meet once a week for breakfast and to ply their wares. The premise is that members of each group find recommendations and work for each other. You have to be a member to go regularly but for the first few weeks, until you submit your membership application, you can go along for free to see if it will serve you. I suggest that you contact your local branch and go along. It is a smorgasbord of delights and I was a member of the Hove Albion branch for some time. The best thing about it is that there are usually representatives of the key trades that you need in that room. They are there every week and over a period of time you will get to know them.

There will usually be an odd-job guy in the group. He can help you with a wide range of tasks and you can get feedback on the quality of his work from the other members of the group. If he has done work for other members of the group and he is still in the group, then the work probably went OK! I suggest that when you find such a person, you sign them up for your project.

You will likely also find a bigger, builder-type in the room who will take on larger projects such as building extensions and things like that. He is also valuable to you because he will have access to the trades you need to get on with your refurbs. Sign him up to your team too

As well as the general builders you need, you might also meet a couple of other key people in the room who can help you. There is always an accountant and there is always a solicitor. In my "Hove Albion chapter" these people were very professional and could definitely assist with property adventures. Sign them up to your team as well.

There is usually also a dentist in the group. I'm not sure how they could help you on your property adventure, but you never know when you might need a new dentist.

Another fantastic resource for finding contractors who can help you with your refurb projects are your local property network meetings. It doesn't really matter which organisation is running the meeting. Of course, my favourite meetings are run by the Progressive Property Network and they are always excellent, but there are other meetings run by different organisations and there are a number of independent ones also. Whoever is running them, make sure that you go along. They generally meet once a month in a local hotel or similar venue. The reason that you have to go is that the people you meet there will be very helpful to you.

You will generally meet local property investors and longstanding landlords who have been there, done it and got the T-shirt. Whatever challenge you face in your new property business, they will have come across it and will have dealt with it. They will know people who can help you. They will likely have a list of reliable contractors and tradesmen in their phonebooks. These lists have been built up over time and if you are on the list then you are usually a decent contractor. Go and speak with these people, have coffee with them, get to know them.

They will be an invaluable resource for you in your new investment and flipping business.

Chapter Fourteen: Flippin' Builders

Of course, looking for builders in the ways described in the previous chapter would usually be the sensible way to do it. Back when we were starting out, we didn't know the sensible way to do it. Instead, we did something different. I wouldn't recommend these ways of finding builders for reasons that will become obvious, but this is what we did.

First we went and sat in the car park at Wickes or B&Q at seven in the morning. That's not quite the same as going to Wickes and B&Q car park at three in the morning and at that time you meet a completely different crew and who would be better discussed in a different book.

At 7am, what you see floating in and out of the car park are little vans owned by local builders who are buying their stock for the day for the jobs they have lined up. You may well think this is a valuable resource but we didn't find that to be the case.

We took their business cards and made a note of where they were working. Where possible we would go and visit them on the job and it was very revealing. The ones that we met as the sun was coming up over B&Q, who we had thought would be good to work with, sometimes turned out to be those we would least like to work with. On the other hand, the ones we didn't immediately take to, often turned out to be really good. What we learned was that it was impossible to judge until we'd visited them on-site.

We got in a terrible mess on some of our refurbs, and some of the strangest and most disappointing things happened.

There was one young man who undertook to do a major project for us in the early days. He had been working away quite diligently and on a particular Friday, the day when all accounts are due and "the lads" have to be paid, he asked us to arrange the next tranche of monies that were due at that point in the project. To be fair to him, the required work at that stage was properly completed so the sum of £7,000 was transferred to his account. We all went off to enjoy the weekend. On Monday morning it was clear that the builder was making a slow start to the week. When we visited the house later that day, nothing was happening. I chased him on the phone and he didn't pick up. After a little while I received a text suggesting that we might meet at the house within the hour. I approached the meeting with some trepidation and it turned out that I was right to do so.

Our man turned up, not in his work clothing, but in smart-casual attire and he brought his little dog along with him too. It was a very pleasant little dog, but I had hoped to see some workmen with him or any sign that things would pick up and the works would recommence shortly. There was bad news. It appears that our favourite builder had jetted off on the previous Friday evening to a "stag do" in Amsterdam. He had taken most of the £7,000 staged payment to continue the refurbishment with him and, I believe the colloquial term is, that he had shoved it up his nose. The money had gone and the refurbishment had ground to a halt. We had to sort that out. Despite all the protestations and promises, it was expensive.

This is the stuff they don't teach you on the property courses.

On another occasion, during another project with another builder, I received a text from the builder at three in the morning to tell me that... he was dead! Some seven hours later I managed to speak with him and he was clearly not dead. I asked him **"What the flip??"**

"Oh Dave, you should have been there. I was slipping away. This bright light was coming towards me. They brought me back from the other side. I thought it was all over... Well anyway I won't be in today"

I had already figured that out for myself, but what I didn't fully grasp at that point is that he wouldn't return to the site at all. Ever.

One of the most difficult things I have found in dealing with builders, is how to deal with the situation where your builder leaves the site in the middle of the job. When that happens, you have to try and find someone to come in and pick up where they left off. The issue here is that the new contractor is very wary about the quality of work that has gone before them. This is especially true if the work is structural and they cannot see the work because it is buried behind newly plastered walls.

If you are doing a light refurb, mainly cosmetic repairs with new flooring or something similar, then this will not be an issue. That is the sort of refurb you should be doing at the start of your property career. As we move forward we tend to take on projects that are bigger and bigger. I urge you not get sucked into doing this unless and until you know exactly what you are doing.

This book is aimed at readers who are at the start of their property adventure and might be on the point of taking on their first project. I know that this may well include readers who come from a building or contracting background, and that is great. You presumably know where the pitfalls are and you should go ahead, but always go ahead cautiously.

For the rest of us, we should all tread carefully.

Sometimes you can unfortunately go wrong even if you actually do all the right things; somehow life intervenes. We were once introduced to a bright young man by one of the estate agents that we had started to work with. We went and visited him on site where we found that the site was a blur of activity. There were happy builders everywhere working away, singing and whistling as they went. The project was moving apace and it reminded me of a one of those Big Build projects you see on the TV. The young man in charge worked with his dad and they had two teams. We were excited and we decided to commit to him.

At that stage we had got a bit, shall we say, over-excited about the scale of the projects we were looking at. At that time we had cut our teeth on the more basic *vanilla* projects and we had decided that were moving up. We were looking to add more value than could be added in a basic flip. We wanted cash-flow from this house and we wanted lots of it.

I am going to pause now for just a second and emphasise that we actually made a real mess of the projects undertaken at this point in our journey. What I am about to share with you cost us money rather than earning us money. Beware if you have thoughts of scaling up too quickly as it can spell trouble for us all.

Getting back to the story; so here was the plan. The young builder had two teams and this was fortunate because we were looking at two projects, both of which were similar in scale. We planned to take two, two-up, two-down Victorian terraced properties and turn them each into five bed Houses of Multiple Occupation (HMO). All rooms were going to be fitted with en-suite shower rooms. This would take the rent roll from around £6,000pa to around £26,000pa. This is of course a massive increase and I have to say we were feeling pretty good about the projects and about ourselves.

The houses were secured, the quotes were obtained and accepted and the start date for the rip outs were put in the diary; the builds began.

What we were not aware of was that the two building teams were almost entirely made up of family and friends. All of them knew each other really well. They had grown up together, gone to school together and spent their time socially together. They all knew each other's business really well and they all knew each other's partners really well. That is where it all started to go wrong, and unhappily for us, this came immediately after they had ripped-out both of our houses. Both houses had everything removed and were now stripped back to brick. There was nothing left, no fixtures, no fittings, no plaster and no internal walls (other than those that were structural). Everything had gone.

To give you an idea just how completely they'd been ripped out, if you walked in through the front door of either house you could see through to the rear wall of the house. If you looked up, you could see into the roof space. This is scary stuff for the new property investor who is not used to taking on projects at this level.

It was at this delicate time in the refurbishment project that we were struck by the unfolding of a really unfortunate series of events. It transpired that one of the tradesmen in one of the teams had been having a secret liaison with the wife of one of the tradesmen in the other building team. Inevitably, as happens in these circumstances, the facts were bound to come out.

Unfortunately for us, the facts came out when we had two houses completely destroyed and taken back to brick. The fallout was immense. The guy who had been caught, left the project and his team, but it didn't stop there. It transpired that other members of the team had known about what was going on. Others affiliated with the various members of the building teams and their partners also got involved, so things got even more fraught and dramatic. It now went something like this; The lady involved in the deception was upset that he had known about her and what she had got up to with him and wasn't happy about them continuing to work together. Meanwhile the wronged-man refused to work any longer with the other guy because he hadn't known anything about it and was upset because he had been left out. Others linked with the builders took sides, accused each other of knowing things and not knowing things, and of leaving each other out. I have probably lost you somewhere in there but you catch my drift. It was a mess and it was a drama.

The result was that everyone had left both sites. The only people who were left were the young man who ran the business and his dad; two people remaining to take on what were two really big projects (for us at least).

If you ever get yourself into this sort of a pickle, then I am going to give you some advice that will serve you well. My biggest problem back then was that I didn't have anyone to give me the advice about what to do at the time.

The advice is to STOP... Stop the project. Stop everything.

We didn't stop. We listened to our contractor who told us he could recruit more tradesmen and still get the jobs finished in the required timescale and we believed him. The truth is, that we wanted to believe him and the reason we wanted to believe him was that we had given him the first tranche of monies for each project so that he could make a start; Ten thousand pounds per property! We were in for 20 grand. 20 large. £20,000.

All we had to show for that significant investment were two houses that, as we saw it, had been destroyed. We didn't want to lose the money.

For this reason, we hung in there and it was a mistake to do so. I believe that the young man tried his best, but he never managed to replace his teams. On several occasions, when he announced that he had managed to recruit replacements, the quality of the new people coming in was just not up to scratch.

The thing to understand is that these projects were quite big and technical and that is why you shouldn't take them on if you are not a builder and you are just starting out. I understand that at one level we were just pulling apart an old house and putting it back together again, but actually what we were doing was very tough. We were taking a house that was over 100 years old and were significantly reconfiguring it and extending it. The kitchens were being extended and we were installing dormer windows in the roof space. Five en-suite shower rooms were to be fitted where before there was only one shared family bathroom in each house. We got involved in stuff that we should never have got involved with. When you take a house that is 130 years old back to brick, all its flaws and issues, previously concealed from generations past, are revealed.

Building control love it. They come in and want you to bring the house up to 21st century standard. With extensions, loft rooms and dormer windows they want you to talk about loading, to install steel beams and complete complex calculations. We didn't know you had to do all of this and such things were not in our thoughts when we came up with the scheme. It was a nightmare made up of delays and added expense.

Unfortunately, most small builders in and around Manchester where we were working at the time underestimated the task and the effort involved. They had been working in this type of property all their working lives and had worked on hundreds of sites. They thought that we couldn't teach them anything about doing refurbs on terraced houses but they were wrong. They couldn't handle the technicalities of doing these kind of projects.

The purpose of me sharing this with you now is to underline the point that if you are new to investing and flipping then you should be very careful regarding what work you take on. Of course we have to add value to make our flips work but you should only take on a project that you know you can finish. Builders will on occasion let you down.

The young builder above lost his team and we were frightened to say to him that we would bring someone else in to finish the job because it would crystallise a loss. We had paid him £20,000 but in truth, at the time everything fell apart he had probably only completed about £10,000 worth of work. If we threw him off the job at that point, then we would have lost the other £10,000. You may say that we should have asked him for a refund, and that would be a logical step to take. However, in the real world things are not that straight forward. He had spent some of the money. He had lost his teams, and in that moment he had lost his business. He didn't have the money to refund to us and was in all likelihood going to fund the ongoing project by leveraging his trade accounts with suppliers and his bank facility.

He tried to soldier on and we were scared to stop him, thinking that we might still finish up okay and not crystallise a debt. Ultimately it ended badly. He couldn't raise enough funds to continue the project properly. He started to take short-cuts on the build and didn't tell us. He just put a brave face on everything, turned up every day with a smile and said everything was all right. We knew he was struggling but we believed him when he told us it would be okay because we wanted to be okay. We had no idea what he had been up to.

Eventually, he announced that he had finished one of the projects so we went and had a look. It looked fine and we had no idea that it wasn't. The paperwork was running a little behind but we didn't think too much of it at the time. Looking back, this should have been a massive red flag for us.

We moved tenants in and only then did we begin to see the scale of the issue. First, we had a few leaks reported to us. A few leaks, soon became a lot of leaks. Then we were told that there were issues in the back yard, and finally we started to get reports of damp issues internally.

The bottom line was that he had duped us. There were leaks because the craftsmanship was so shoddy that the joints in the white plastic pipework that ran like a maze under floors, above ceilings and behind walls had started to pop and to leak. This represented a serious expense for us to sort out. When we investigated the damp patches internally, we found that he had never fitted a new damp proof course. It was on the specification of works and we had paid for it but he never actually did the work. It took months before we realised the scale of the problem and to resolve it we had to strip down walls and start all over again. We lost tenants, we lost time and we lost money.

It was the issues in the back yard that we found the most shocking. Ultimately this was the easiest to fix but on the day we discovered what he had done, we were completely dumbstruck. He had run the waste from five ensuite bathrooms out of the house into the back yard down to ground level and then he had stopped. Building control had advised an upgrade of the drainage with new inspection hatches should be included, but he had done none of this. The bottom line was that we had a back yard that was filling up with poo; not nice. It was not nice for the tenants, Not nice for the neighbours and a bit scary for us. We were devastated.

All the above issues were eventually sorted out. We rolled our sleeves up and found builders locally who could help, but this time we did it the right way. We went to Check-a-Trade, we sought referrals and recommendations and we found some honest, genuine builders who felt sorry for us and decided to help.

The other factor at play here was quite interesting to experience, and is also and worthy of a mention. It appears that genuine builders are also aware of rogue builders and they take it, to an extent, as their responsibility to right the wrongs and clear up the messes that their colleagues in the industry have left behind. Our new builders came in and took on jobs that in normal circumstances they would never have taken on. They did it because they recognised that an injustice had been done by one of their fellow builders.

There was a price to pay of course, since we were paying for the same jobs twice and we were paying for the disruption. We had withheld a final payment from the original builder pending all the paperwork, but to be honest that was not enough. We had also never considered the fact that we had also released funds to him to complete the second project. That then became an issue for us also, because at this point he had just disappeared, leaving us with a half-finished project of questionable quality there as well.

Once again, we involved our new best-friend builders who had rescued us on the first project, to help us on the second one. Again there was duplication of cost and we finished up way over budget but at least we avoided the worst aspects of the unpleasant first project, and eventually got everything finished.

What are the lessons learned here? The first is that in terms of building projects and refurbs, you have no idea what you are doing until you have done a few or you have received some training and knowledge in how to do it.

Do not do what I did! On this occasion learning by doing is a very expensive way to learn.

The next lesson is one that I have learned more than once in my business life over the decades but on this occasion I didn't apply it. This isn't because I forgot the lesson, but rather because I didn't recognise its relevance as the saga was unfolding. The lesson is that if you have gone into a deal that has gone wrong and ultimately you are going to suffer a loss, then your first loss will be the cheapest. What we should have done, and what you should do if you find yourself in a similar position, is to stop the project when it starts to go wrong and crystallise the debt at that point. Admittedly we would have lost £10,000 if we'd done this in this project, but our ultimate loss was higher because we carried on. We also spent months trying to sort it all out. It dominated our lives while we could have spent that time far more productively moving our business forward.

The other great advantage we would have had at that point was that the buildings were complete shells. They had been stripped back to brick and everything had been ripped out; no electrics, no plumbing, no kitchen, no bathroom, no nothing. At the time, I thought that this was a problem but in fact it was to our advantage if we were going to bring in new contractors to pick up the job. They could see everything and they wouldn't have been in a position where they were picking up someone else's work, where they had no idea to what standard it had been done. It would actually have been easier for a new contractor to step in at that point. I thought mistakenly thought it would be harder, so I clung on to the original guy. I was wrong.

You can learn from me.

Chapter Fifteen: Sourcing The Deal

Let's now assume that you know where you are going to buy and you have started to put a power team together. It is now time to get out there and start looking for property. You need to buy something that you can add value to, and that is the same criteria whether you are buying to keep or if you are looking to flip.

There are a few major resources for sourcing houses. The ones I am going to deal with here are those that will give you the fastest results with the least effort if you are just starting out. I am going to talk about sourcing from estate agents or from auctions. These are the resources that you will see on the TV programmes that talk about buying investment property and buying to add value so that you can sell at a profit, so these are the places I am going to deal with here. That excludes a whole list of possibilities for prospecting deals based on the Direct to Vendor basis. There are many property professionals who use these methods and dark arts to find some fantastic deals but in truth they are certainly at a more advanced level than most of us just starting out. As such, maybe that's material best suited for another book, or something you can learn about in someone else's book who specialises in that area. My job here and now is to get you started quickly and for free.

To start your search, you must go into your local estate agent. In fact, you must go into all of them. You don't know at this point which one is likely to build a relationship with you, so go and see all of them, tell them what you are doing and tell them what you are looking for. Be completely transparent and open with them as they cannot help you if you don't tell them what you want. You will get a mixed response to start with since most estate agents have heard it all before. They have had thousands of people who have come into their offices because they have watched TV programmes where people made some money out of property, and believe that they can do it too.

As they will learn, you are different for you will be educated. They just don't know that you are different, yet.

The most important thing that you need to show for an estate agent to bring you the best deals, is to show that you can pay for it. If there is a mythical black book of investors that the estate agent will send their best deals to, then there is no reason why you cannot be on it.

You just have to be serious, and be prepared to buy.

Chapter Sixteen:
Viewing The Houses

The next step in the process is to go on viewings. There is an art to doing viewings and once you know what you are looking for it can be quite a short process. At one point in our development as property investors and sourcers, we were looking for a particular type of property with a particular footprint and near particular amenities. We had to find houses that were big enough to become five bed, all en-suite Houses of Multiple Occupancy (HMO).

We perfected what we called the "seven-second" viewing and I think the name was inspired by a film that was very popular at that time. Of course it wasn't really a viewing in seven seconds as it took way longer than that. The seven seconds didn't include the drive to the property, which could have been as long as 30 minutes from our base, nor the 30-minute drive back again. It certainly didn't include the standing around in the street waiting for the agents' viewing person who had the keys. That could be another 15 minutes.

Finding the keys of course was a totally different issue. In my experience the viewing person would normally be a slightly older person, possibly retired, or a very young person who was doing this job for the day because somebody had to, and they were the most junior in the branch. Keys were certainly an issue. Typically, the viewing person would be visiting several properties during the day and would have set off in the morning with as many as 20 sets of keys for the day in their car. By the time they got to us, the key chains were less than organised. It invariably took them several minutes to locate the correct set of keys. Then having grabbed the right set it would take several minutes more, accompanied by a suitable amount of huffing and puffing, shoving and tutting to locate which key on that key ring would actually open the front door. They would look at us triumphantly and beckon us forward.

We would enter the property, have a quick scan of the ground floor rooms, see they were clearly too small and leave the property again before the viewing person had a chance to extract the key from the front door lock and follow us in. "Thank you" we said and would set off to the car leaving them looking slightly puzzled.

So there you are, another seven-second viewing but on this occasion it was one which had taken the best part of an hour and a half.

We were not always as efficient at doing the viewings. In the early days it was a much more dawn out affair.

My business partner seemed to take the lead on this. I don't know why, it was just something that happened. Most of the time I would bowl up in the morning and he would tell me we were off to some God-forsaken place on the map that was nowhere near our goldmine area. At first, I questioned this broad-brush approach that he took but we had reached the point where I just went along for a quiet life.

He pushed me a little too far one weekend when he told me that he had booked a viewing at a terraced property in Burnley at 10am on Monday morning. There were two issues with this news. First, I had been to Burnley before and I didn't like it. I don't mention this out of a sense of being disrespectful to the citizens of that grand old town that is Burnley, but for my purposes, for buying investment property and looking for flips, then it didn't really float my boat.

It had been a wet and windy Tuesday afternoon in Greater Manchester and we had no viewings in the diary. A prospective investor client had let us down and cancelled his appointment with us for a little tour of our projects and the weather was awful. We were at a loose end and ordinarily I am a big fan of loose ends. I would have had no problem in going back to our apartment in order to tidy up some emails and maybe squeeze in a bit of a power nap. But no… it appeared that another agenda was in the air.

"Let's go to Burnley" DG announced.

"Why?"

The answer was never really forthcoming, but it had clearly been decided. It was probably the result of one of his phone conversations with another wholesale property trader, probably of ill-repute, who had told him that Burnley was the place to be and that the streets were paved with gold.

We set off, but I was not happy. I understand that there are pleasant parts of Burnley but we had been directed to very specific parts of postcodes BB10 and BB11, areas which were not pleasant. The streets looked run down and fairly deserted except for several large groups of youngsters, all of whom were wearing hooded tops and all of whom I suspected were up to no good. The weather was awful, the rain was tipping down and the whole place was grey and foreboding in the way that only an East Lancashire town can be during what was a glorious summer's day elsewhere in the United Kingdom.

I refused to get out of the car as something in my gut told me that this was not for me and in terms of our property career this would end badly. In the event my gut instinct turned out to be proven correct but I will come back to this.

A few minutes passed with me still sitting in the car and with DG reminding me of all the times I had been wrong over the years (to be fair there were a few). He reminded me that "I should take a more positive attitude to the business especially when he had-had what he thought was a great idea." He laboured that I was "just so negative and how depressing it was for him to try to be an uplifting, positive, inspired, inspirational leader all the time if all I was going to do was sit there and subject him to such negative waves".

In the end I relented and agreed to investigate further, if only to stop him going on and on, and in order that our normal state of frosty silence might return.

We had no idea where to go, so we made a beeline for the corner shop which turned out to be a café. The menu was limited and it turned out to be full English breakfast, but you could order and have it served in various sizes starting from £2.99. A very reasonable midday treat.

You can learn a lot from sitting in a place like this. You can watch the footfall in the street. You can try to enrol the owner into conversation and try to pick up tit-bits of information with respect to local estate agents or possibly builders that you might be able to work with. You can get an idea about the local community just by watching the customers come and go over a few minutes. It was in relation to the local community that we got what was a deep insight into the type of person that lived in BB10 and BB11.

A man came into the café and shook off the rain from his coat.

"How much is the Full English?" he said

"£5.99 with toast and tea".

"I haven't got £5.99"

"Well I can do a smaller one for £2.99"

"I haven't got £2.99"

"Well how much have you got?"

"I've got 99p. What can I have for 99p?"

Well at this stage the café owner clearly felt sorry for this potential customer and although nothing was said between us, we all understood that he had chosen this moment to do something kind and to help a stranger whom he felt had fallen on hard times and clearly needed a meal.

"Ah, well for 99p, I can do you an egg, a sausage and a bit of bacon all served with a cup of tea"

A random act of kindness for a stranger who had entered the café owner's life and from whom he sought nothing in return. You would think that a suitably grateful word of thanks would have been appropriate but that is not what he got:

"Can I have an extra egg?"

You clearly can't please all of the people all of the time!

Getting back to our 10am Monday morning appointment with an estate agent in a house in Burnley. Normally it wouldn't have been an issue but remember we live in Brighton and we would be spending the preceding weekend in Brighton. That is a drive of some 300 miles and some six hours on the road if you are lucky. On the Sunday evening DG messaged me to let me know that he would pick me up at 4am on the Monday morning to ensure that we were in Burnley on time for the viewing. The car pulled up on the stroke of 4am and I was waiting behind the living room curtains. I climbed into the car seething with rage that my life had been disrupted to this extent and also because DG kept wittering away as he drove or kept turning the radio on and off and then decided to sing along merrily to his cherished CD of Dusty Springfield's Greatest Hits. It appeared that he had made the decision that if he had to stay awake in the car then so would everyone else, meaning me. My rage continued unabated because as well as the enforced sing-along I had real suspicions that BB10 and BB11 were not going to be great places for us to invest and also that this particular house would be a dog.

We didn't speak until we had passed Stoke. The sun came up while we were in Keele Services taking a comfort break. On the chime of 10am we turned the corner into the rather depressing and run-down street in Burnley where this investment opportunity was located. We could see that already waiting for us were a young man from the estate agent who had opened the house

www.getintoproperty.co.uk | 95

up, along with our favourite contractor of all time, Tony, who had agreed to meet us to help us assess the potential of this investment.

Sitting in the front of the car, from about 100 yards away I made eye contact with Tony. His face was downcast and he was shaking his head from side to side. That was enough for me. I instantly knew that this property was not one to add to our portfolio and that Tony would have good reason for giving me the sign.

However, DG's enthusiasm for this project knew no bounds and he skipped from the car. He was determined, it seemed to me, to rise above my lethargy and lack of commitment to the cause and to prove me wrong. I have to say he looked the part. He had shared with me, between Stoke and Keele services, that he had spent the weekend with the lovely Mrs DG at Bicester Outlet Mall where he had made some canny purchases for his wardrobe and at a healthy discount. This particular morning, now that it was light and the fog in my head had cleared, I could see that he was sporting a brand new Boss dark jacket in the style that was worn on the touchline with such elegance by Sir Alex Ferguson, together with a very sharply pointed pair of shoes which were made out of the skin of some poor and unsuspecting dead animal and which made a "clip-clopping" noise as he walked along the pavement. He leapt ahead of me with abandon. I shuffled along behind, completely disinterested.

DG hailed the lad from the estate agent with a hearty well-met as if they were long lost friends and they stepped off together briskly to do the viewing. I held back and spoke to Tony.

"What's the problem Tony?"

"It's a shocker. There are decades of no maintenance, poor maintenance, DIY disasters, botch-ups and everything. But it's more than that. I'm not sure that it's safe David"

"OK. Well we'll let him have a look. He knows what he's doing"

Tony looked at me disbelieving.

Meanwhile the viewing was going apace. We couldn't hear every word but there was a lot of *"Ooooh-ing"* and *"Ahhhh-ing"*. I am sure I heard DG say at one point *"Ah yes... this could be a game changer"*. All the while, these positive words were accompanied by the constant clip clop of his new "bargain" shoes.

He was above us now. Tony and I had shuffled into the front room which was entered directly off the street. We went in to shelter from the wind but DG was definitely directly above us and clip clopping across what I assumed would be a bedroom; I never went to look as it turned out. As he trotted happily across the bedroom we heard a strange creaking noise in the house. I didn't know what it was but I am sure that you will understand when I say that it was not a *good* noise. I think we all instinctively understand the difference between a good noise and a bad noise. This was a bad noise.

Suddenly there was a rush of air and a crash. As we stood in the front room, time stood still as DG's left leg crashed through the ceiling above us closely followed by his right leg. It seemed for a moment that everything was over and the worst had passed as he, in a state of some surprise, dangled his pointy shoes backwards and forwards across the front room ceiling. I ran upstairs to help him escape his predicament, but had sadly arrived too late. It appeared that his fall from grace had only been held up momentarily. It was only the thickness of his new coat, of admittedly great quality which had held him in place and had temporarily prevented his inevitable fall to the floor below.

By the time I reached the room above it was too late. He had crashed downwards into the front room. I ran back down the stairs again and expected to see him on the floor in the front room, but I couldn't actually see anything at all. There was dust and a fog of lathe and plaster and rubbish filling the room. Gradually I could make out two little eyes peering out at me and so I asked a really silly question:

"Are you alright?"

"No I am not all right! Get me out of here"

We extricated him from the rubble.

"Can I get you anything?"

"Get me a brandy!"

And this from a man who does not drink, at just gone 10am on a Monday morning, a man who had just done his best to single-handedly destroy a hundred-year-old terraced house in Burnley.

We headed for A&E but there were no lasting injuries other than to his pride. The same cannot be said of the new Boss jacket and the pointy clip clop shoes. Collateral damage - I never saw them again.

That wasn't the only time that we finished up in A&E after a viewing. There had been an incident several months earlier in Oldham but on that occasion the property had real potential. This was a big house which was a perfect fit to our criteria. We were doing the viewing with an agent that we hadn't worked with before and on this occasion it was the branch manager who had met with us. This was exciting because if we could make a good impression then it would cement our relationship and could open the door for who knows how many more projects to be offered to us.

This house was huge. It had a loft room, which had been properly built with building control approval and everything. It even had a basement.

On this occasion I went upstairs and DG went to investigate the basement. He carefully eased his way on to the wooden staircase just inside the door to the basement and looked for the light switch. It was dark and he was searching on the wall just with his fingers hoping that through his sense of touch he could locate the switch. Still no light switch was found. He ventured on another step downward feeling along the wall as he went. Nothing. One more step and he would surely find it and as he gingerly moved forward he felt into his pocket for his phone because he knew that there was a torch on his phone. At this point his world was turned upside down, literally. There were no more steps even though he was only about half way down to the basement floor. In the dark he completed a double somersault, piked with a 2.5 twist, a dive that a young Tom Daly in his prime would have been proud of. He landed on the hard stone floor of the basement.

I heard the cry and ran to assist.

"Can you get me out of here!" the words came from the darkness.

"To be honest... no I can't."

There was just half a staircase, no rope, no ladder, no nothing. I had no idea how to get him out especially if he had hurt himself.

"Why didn't you warn us?" I asked the estate agent.

"I didn't know" he said *"I'm calling an ambulance"*.

The ambulance duly arrived, by which time I had borrowed a ladder from a neighbour and DG was on his feet. Again no lasting damage had been done but, of course, we did not know that at the time.

Our relationship building exercise with that estate agent faltered somewhat on that afternoon and never really recovered. I think that its fate was sealed when, as the ambulance door was closing to whisk us away to A&E, he pushed his head round the door and asked:

"Will you be making an offer?"

Chapter Seventeen: Sourcing The Deal – Auctions

The other main way that newcomers into the industry tend to source properties to purchase or to flip is through auctions. I blame the TV programmes for this trend and if you watch *Homes Under the Hammer* or the like, they make it look easy. Buying at auction is not necessarily easy.

That said, it can be easy but you have to know what you are doing and you have to do your due diligence beforehand. For the first time auction buyer, this is how I suggest that you start.

The first step is to go along to a couple of auctions to understand how it all works. Do not bid, just watch the process and see how the professionals do it. Do not be tempted to bid on a house during these reconnaissance trips, as you need to do the viewings and all the background work before you start bidding.

The first time I went to an auction to try to buy a specific property, I made all the classic schoolboy errors. I asked my estate agent friend to come along with me to *help me*. It didn't really help because ultimately I had to make the decisions since I was the one paying for the building. I had been a bit nervous about how the auction worked, so I sought comfort in him holding my hand on the day. It cost me £200 for his time so I went on my own in future.

It didn't occur to me for a moment that he might know the auctioneer really well through business and socially. The auctioneer came over to say hello before the auction started. By the time the conversation had finished he knew exactly who we were, why we were there, what lot we were interested in and roughly how much we were prepared to pay. I didn't mean to tell him those things but it kind of came out during the conversation he had with my estate agent. I also got the impression that he already knew who we were and why we were there, which was kind of weird.

When the auction started, we chose to sit in the front row. When you attend an auction NEVER sit in the front row. You always sit or stand at the back of the room. Why? So you can see what is going on around the room. We were stuck at the front and if I am honest, there seemed to be an inordinate amount of interest in our lot. People appeared to be bidding from all over the room. This struck me as strange. Allow me to explain. This was still at a time when I had a retail business and we had a shop in a parade a shops in a strong secondary position. The freeholder of the block put the whole block up for sale as individual units and several of them were offered for sale on this particular day.

The point is that these shop units were pretty much identical in size and there are about 12 or so in the block. We were the only existing tenant who came to the auction with the intention of buying the long lease; a 999-year lease and a virtual freehold interest. The other traders in the parade didn't come.

All the units were sold subject to the existing leases so all the traders would be secure, but the carrot that had lured us to the auction was the possibility of acquiring a virtual freehold interest. Our knowledge of property at that time was limited but we did know that the acquisition of an asset like this, over time, would transform our balance sheet for the better. Furthermore, as the value of the asset rose in future, we could use it to secure lending from our banks. Maybe this was not something the other traders wanted to do. Maybe they couldn't raise the money. Who knows?

We sat through several lots and the auction was quite active. When we finally got to the point in the auction where this parade of shops was offered, bidding was very quiet and there didn't seem to be a lot of interest in our block of shops. Some of the units in the parade didn't even sell, but then we got to our unit.

From what I had seen, interest in these small units was very limited. The prices offered were quite low and I was quite excited that we might buy our unit at a very reasonable price. However, as soon as our unit was offered, bidding took off apace. I couldn't see who was bidding since I was stuck at the front. I couldn't turn around and look at the crowd to try to spot who it was as you just don't do that. We kept bidding and the opposition kept bidding right back, but we still kept bidding further. We hadn't come all this way to lose the deal and we had allowed ourselves to get emotional about our choice which was another mistake. The bidding reached a level that none of the other units in the block had achieved and eventually the bidding exceeded our target offer. We kept going until the gavel came down; we had bought the most expensive shop unit on the parade.

That is how not to do it. Let me help any of you who are setting out to do it for the first time, to do it right.

This is what you *should* do, in the order that you should do it.

The first step is to go online and register with all the auction houses that operate in your area. There will be the occasional time when a property in your area is offered by an auction house that is not in your area and you will not see it if you aren't registered with that particular auction house. You just have to keep your eyes and ears open. Usually the bigger auction houses have an auction every couple of months. They will publish the catalogue online first, and when they do, you can download the catalogue and trawl through it. At this point we have spent no money.

You may find a couple of properties in the catalogue that you like the look of in which case you should ring the auction house and book a viewing. It is likely that they will have allocated three or four specific times and dates for the viewings and you have to be available at those times and dates to view the house. It is also likely that you will not be viewing alone and that they will be group viewings. Other people who may have an interest in the house will be there and you shouldn't be put off or intimidated by this; most of the people you see on the viewing won't end up bidding. By the time that you get to the auction room you will have just a few people bidding and they are your true competition, not the people at the viewing.

You should also ensure that you download the legal pack from the auction house. This is a very important document which contains details of all legal issues and threats relating to ownership to the property. You may not feel that you are qualified to fully digest the material and in truth, if you are just starting out then you probably aren't. You should show it to a solicitor. There is a cost to this, but it is way cheaper to get advice at this stage than to get it wrong and only find out after the event. The other thing you need to factor in is that your solicitor might be busy. They do have other clients of course, and in those circumstances you have to act quickly so that you receive the advice you need before the auction.

The auction day has now arrived. Here is where you should be in terms of preparation for the sale: You have spotted a property and you have been to view it. You have read the legal pack and have sought advice where you need it. Now you have to look at the numbers.

The numbers will be different dependent on where you are based. In the North West my numbers were very well defined. I had to buy the house cheaply enough to allow me to pay all the costs of acquisition plus any refurbishment and upgrades that I had planned. I then had to look at selling costs and factor those in too. Once all of that was factored in, I needed to buy the house at a price so that I would make a margin of 20% net on my investment. That meant that if a property costed me a total of £100,000, then I need to walk away with a profit of £20,000 net. It also gave me an indication of my buying price. Experience taught me over time, that when you are buying a property to flip then your highest bid has to be no more than 60p in the £ of the final refurbished value of the property. If you pay any more than this, then usually your margin will be threatened and the project may not give you a decent profit.

What do I mean by 60p in the £ of the refurbished value? Well in this example it is quite straight forward. In this example I am hoping to generate a re-sale of the updated refurbished property at £120,000. Therefore, as a rule of thumb I need to purchase at around £72,000. My profit is to be £20,000. The remaining £28,000 will be what is required to pay all transaction costs, taxes including Stamp Duty, fees to buy, fees to sell, finance costs, refurbishment costs and every other cost that I might incur.

A 20% return can be quite challenging to achieve, wherever you are based in the UK. If you are buying a higher value property, then you may move away from the "60p in the £" rule and look instead for a bespoke profit figure for that particular deal. For instance, 20% profit on a £500,000 house is a large profit. You may be happy to work for less in those circumstances and decide that maybe a £50,000 profit might suffice in that case, but you must be very careful. You need to be very realistic in the predictions for your figures to ensure that the deal works.

Whatever margin you are looking for, the best way to make sure that you get a great result is to do your calculations with respect to the figures based on three separate outcomes for the figure achievable on re-sale.

The first outcome would be if you buy at your figure, the refurb runs to plan to the penny and then you get your selling price. This would be the perfect scenario and you would secure the maximum return on the project. Other things that may happen in this scenario might be that the sun would shine every day forever, your life would be full of happy, smiley faces at all times, I might win the British Open Golf Championship and West Ham United win the Premiership.

You then need to base your figures on a scenario where it is cold rainy and miserable, all the news on the TV is bad, the property market has taken a sudden dive whilst you were in the middle of this project, tumbleweed is blowing up the High Street with the economy in decline and West Ham United still win the Premiership.

Finally, you must do your calculations based on figures that are achievable, realistic and unsurprising. Find a number in the middle that you believe will be achieved and then have a look and see if you have still achieved your 20% margin.

You will soon get an idea as to whether the project will work, but it is very important to do all three calculations to make sure you have an overview of the numbers in each scenario. Do it exactly as I have written it above and that will keep you safe.

Once you have the numbers pretty well set in your head, then you can work out what to bid. You will have a maximum figure that you can go to in the bidding in order to make the project work. Do NOT exceed that figure. The issue is that once the bidding takes off, you may be tempted to go a little bit further to try to secure your deal. I understand this feeling and I have done it myself.

This is poor practise and you have to be disciplined. If you have completed the exercise above, then you will know how much you can bid. There is a reason why that is the number, and if you exceed it then the viability of the project is threatened. At the very least your profit will be reduced. Don't get suckered in, as there is always another deal.

You are now ready. Go along to the auction room. If you are planning to bid, then you will need to register with the auctioneer's team. They will take you details and give you a paddle with your name on which you will raise to make a bid. It is a very definite process to make a bid, so do not worry about the mythical tales of scratching your nose absentmindedly and having to buy a house as a result. You have to make a concerted effort to be seen. In a busy room, the auctioneer might not even see you for a moment or two. However, he will have assistants around the room who will see you and will guide him to you. I say him because in my experience the role of auctioneer seems to be dominated by men although I don't know why that should be. My apologies to all the lady auctioneers that I haven't seen in action to this point.

Another resource that you will be introduced to at registration are the professional teams that are brought in by the auctioneer to assist prospective purchasers in the room. Of course, you will already have put your power team together and will have everything you need in place, but I always find it interesting to speak to the firms who have come along to support the sale. You will typically encounter solicitors, mortgage brokers, property insurance specialists and local bridging companies. The local bridging firms are particularly interesting because they have great experience in their field. Many of these are family run operations and with their help, many millionaires have been made over a period of time. You should speak to them, since useful alliances can be formed.

Back to the room.

The lot you are interested in bidding on has arrived. Should you jump in at the beginning or should you just sit back and watch and wait to see how it goes? There is no right or wrong here.

Some say you should get in early, declare your serious intent to the room in no uncertain terms and frighten off the opposition with your determination. I tend to take a different view. I will wait to see what happens and watch who is bidding – remember you are standing at the back to get a great view. At some stage the bidding will slow down and there may only be two bidders left in the race. One of them may be starting to become more thoughtful between bids. That is the time to join in. The psychology of this is that suddenly you have revealed yourself as a new bidder and the person who has become more thoughtful will be demoralised because they are near their maximum bid for the lot. Now, maybe for the first time they see that they cannot win. On the other hand, the other bidder was feeling quite happy because they too could see that the opposition had slowed down, but now suddenly you have revealed your hand and they are going to have to beat you down if they are going to win the property. This is a great place for you to be.

Chief Executive Officer In Charge Of Auction Acquisitions

I learned all of this by doing, because I had no access to anyone who could offer me insight on how to do it correctly. When we started out we had to learn this stuff ourselves and we learned in the school of hard knocks. The issue was that at the time it was a rising market and we were not finding enough stock, so we thought that we had to find another way. As a result, I appointed myself as the Chief Officer in charge of Auction Acquisitions. Maybe we could get enough stock there?

I quickly found that this wasn't going to work very well either. Traditionally auctions were the places where property professionals plied their trade and they were not a place for amateurs. If you wanted to find a deal you could find one there, but you needed to take care because these were shark infested waters. It was also the place where property professionals got rid of their mistakes.

In the early 2000's the issue was that all the TV watching property heroes turned up at the auctions and started bidding. There was a rapidly rising property market. Inspired by Sarah, Kirsty and Phil, the butcher, the baker, and the candlestick maker all turned up at the auctions and started bidding. No longer was this reserved space the preserve of the hardened property professional quietly plying his or her trade and nicking stuff for a song to earn their crust. Prices at auctions were now equivalent to retail. The unsophisticated general public were bidding way too much for very ordinary properties. Auction houses were no longer wholesale, trade environments, they were definitely retail with prices sometimes going higher than on the high street. They remained places full of danger and potential disaster for the untrained property investor.

Never was this more fully illustrated to me than when a good property friend of mine, Josh, invited me to join him at an imminent property auction which was to be held at the Old Trafford cricket ground in Manchester, where he had a house entered in the catalogue for sale.

"I have a lot for sale. It should come on after lunch at around 2pm. We can meet for lunch beforehand. I will set a table under the stand"

I had no idea what this meant but on the day I set off for the cricket ground. I parked the car and went in search of lunch. I messaged Josh for directions to find him, and he guided me to a particular spot. I was a bit taken aback at what I saw. There, under one of the grandstands, was a table set up immaculately dressed and covered with a white table cloth surrounded by a selection of folding chairs. We were seated directly beneath a section of seats and these arched over us disappearing into the top of the stand somewhere. There had clearly been some serious shopping done for lunch and the table was set with everything you could imagine, freshly purchased from a local delicatessen. Around the table I found Josh and five or six of his pals whom I did not know, but they all knew each other very well. I thought little of it, enjoyed a super lunch and then watched in admiration as everything, lunch, tablecloth, table and chairs were packed away with military precision as if we had never been there. How cool!

We wandered slowly down to the auction, me, Josh and his pals. The auction got into flow again after the lunch break and Josh's lot was ready to go. I watched with interest. Josh had only recently purchased this property from an estate agent who I knew and was working with. The agent had, in fact offered the property to me but I had declined this opportunity. It was un-mortgageable and was in a terrible state, a liability and no asset. Josh had paid £38,000 for it which sounds cheap but it needed a huge amount spending on it and came with assorted infestations and structural issues; not a project I was keen to take on. Josh paid cash and put it straight into the auction.

Things started slowly but then bids started coming in. There was something very familiar about the people who were bidding. They were scattered all around the room but they were all Joshua's friends who had been at lunch and I was spellbound. What was going on? Up and up the price went. It was now over £80,000. Suddenly there was a new bidder - £85,000 was bid and from someone in the room who was not at the lunch. All the bidding immediately stopped. Josh's pals who had been bidding frantically against each now seemed to just disappear and their interest in the lot had evaporated. The lot was sold to the new bidder.

Of course the buyer had to put down 10% of the price on the day and then in the terms and conditions of the offer had 28 days to complete the purchase. It turned out that he couldn't arrange finance in the time available because of the shocking structural condition of the property. He couldn't raise the funds to complete the purchase. The purchaser had come along to the auction with the intention of buying something else but had failed as the price for his favourite lot went too high. He had stayed on in the room as a spectator and then this lot, Josh's lot, took his attention. He hadn't viewed it and he hadn't read the legal pack. He hadn't done his due diligence and had just bid on the spur of the moment hoping to bag an unexpected bargain. An emotional bid.

Thirty days later the bidder lost his deposit. Joshua got the £8,500 and still owned the property. I was fascinated. It turned out that Josh and his pals repeated the episode again in the very next auction where the house sold again, this time for £80,000 and this time the buyer had the funds to complete in due course. I learned something that day and I have shared the lesson with you now.

Unless you know exactly what you are doing, take care when you buy a property in an auction. If you are new to property, then take this advice. Follow the process that I have laid down above and you will be fine, but do not risk bidding on an auction lot unless you know everything you can learn about the specific property.

The situation can be exacerbated if you find a property that is offered, for instance, in a London auction but is sited some 200 miles away in a Northern town. The question you should ask is why that house is offered in that remote auction room? Sometimes this may well be that it is a mistake that someone else has made and they are just trying to offload it. They cannot offload it locally because all that is needed is the most cursory of viewings to see that this is not a worthy investment. If they place it in a London auction there are two advantages. The first is that no-one is likely to view it. The second is that it might catch someone's attention as a bit of a "punt". Maybe they are sitting in the auction room and are a bit bored. Maybe they will think that relative to London prices the property is a steal. How bad can it be, they may ask themselves? But for £38,000 you can't buy anything inside the M25, so "Let's give it a go" they may reason. A pretty expensive decision, however you look at it.

Chapter Eighteen: Flip To Auction – Selling In Auction

You can sell in property in an auction, and I am happy to sell in an auction as it's much easier than buying. In fact, I quite enjoy the process.

Flipping houses, when you are starting out or when you are more advanced, is about profit; the bottom line is all you need to care about. The classic flip deal is a combination of buying at the right price, adding value by refurbishing it, and then selling at a profit. As with any strategy, there are challenges to ensure you make the maximum profit. If you are using a builder you might experience delays, and if these occur then the project might go over budget. If the project goes over budget, then your bottom line is affected and your profit is reduced. A further consideration is the time-line. To purchase, refurbish and re-sell through an agent can take time. A lot of time. You need to pitch your final retail price correctly to make sure you get viewings and offers that lead to a sale, and this in turn can take a bit of negotiation with the agent that you are selling through, even before you put it back on the market. I recommend that if you bought the house through an agent then you should re-market through the same agent as this will help.

You must make sure that the agent's idea of the value of the finished, newly-upgraded product aligns with yours and will lead to a pretty quick re-sale. In any event, you are probably going to have to wait for nine to 12 months from the time you bought the house before you get it sold and bank the profit. You may be wondering why this is? The answer is because of what is known as the six-month rule. The six-month rule is not actually a rule, but it is a convention applied by most mortgage providers and it has been introduced since the credit crunch of 2008. The bottom line is most lenders will not lend on a house that has not been owned by the vendor for less than six months. It is intended to prevent a distortion of the price by some over-creative property flippers which led to distorted mortgage borrowing before

2008. Just a few bad people exploited the system and they have spoiled it for everyone else. What this means in practice is that, with most lenders, we have to wait at least six-months to sell a refurbished house.

What if there was another way? What if we could earn almost the same margin on our flip by adjusting the model? What if we switched from Buy, Refurb, Sell to…

Buy, DON'T Refurb, Sell

Let me explain how this works. I followed this system recently to earn nearly £20,000 in 20 days without doing any refurb at all and any flipper worth their salt needs to know how this system works.

A recent project on mine was a three bed semi-detached house in a very smart Cul-de-Sac in Greater Manchester.

I went to visit one of my favourite estate agents in Moston to see if he had any stock worth viewing.

"Well you might be interested in this David, it has just fallen through for the second time."

Was I interested? Absolutely I was! Whenever I hear of a house sale falling through for the second time then I am very interested to hear why as it usually earns me some money. On this occasion there were a couple of reasons why, and it was in truth, quite a sad story. The house was owned by Mum. It had been a family home for over 50 years and the family had owned the house from new. Unfortunately, Mum, who was now living in the house alone had become ill and needed to go into full time care. The sons and daughter were now living elsewhere, scattered around the United Kingdom and had their own lives.

The only asset mum owned was the house. She had very little cash and this had disappeared very rapidly when she became ill and had to be moved into a local care home.

When I came along the family were getting desperate and they needed to sell the house because at the time I met them they were paying £800 per week out of post-tax income to keep mum in the home. This was extremely painful and could not be sustained. There were a couple of reasons why the house had not sold. What was not apparent at first sight was that there was an issue with the title of the property, in that the house was not registered at Land Registry which is a requirement now in order for the vendor to sell it. The vendor has to "prove title" in the legal process and without it being registered at Land Registry this was going to take time and be tricky to do.

My surprise at stumbling upon this was that no-one involved seemed to know how to fix it. The family didn't know, but in fairness they were not property people. They were great people and were trying to help their mum but, in my view they were being let down by their advisors. The estate agent didn't know how to fix it and this surprised me, but that is the thing about estate agents; they don't know what they don't know.

What really surprised me was that the family solicitor didn't appear to know how to fix it either, nor did he appear to have any interest in doing so. This was really puzzling but it appeared to fall into context when I was later to find, to my extreme annoyance and frustration that he had set up his practice so that he would only respond to letters. He wouldn't respond to email nor take any phone calls. An astonishing stance in the 21st century and just to reinforce the point if you haven't picked it up already, this is why you need to work with property based solicitors who know what to do and who work within the required timescales. You don't want this man in your property power team.

I did know how to fix this, since I'd come across it before. What you need is for a surveyor to come and do a precise plan of the plot the house stands on with detailed measurements of the plot, the house and any other buildings that you might find on the site. Then you need a draftsman to convert that information into a plan at the required scale of 1:500 with a red line marking the exterior boundary of the plot. There also has to be a compass guide on the drawing showing where North is. You then send the plan to Land Registry with the appropriate documentation and ask them to register the property. Full guidance on how to do this can be found on the Land Registry website.

In order to move things along, I commissioned the drawing. Unfortunately, the process of registration itself was conducted by the painfully slow solicitor (Slow & Co.!) so that held things up a bit, but the normal timescale is that from the time at which Land Registry receives that drawing, it should be a maximum of ten weeks before the title deeds are updated. In my experience Land Registry are very efficient. This job took a bit longer because Slow & Co. had sat on the file for a time before sending it off, in spite of our trying to push them by phone and email, but of course they didn't respond. In due course the title was updated. The total cost of this was about £400 for the survey and the drawing of the plans. I had paid this, and I gave the drawings to the family as a gift. They had needed some help because the sale of the house had come to a complete standstill and they were pouring money into their mum's care.

Once the house was sold, they could then take some of their money back and once the balance on mum's monies had reduced below a certain level, I believe that it was £16,000 at the time, then the state would pick up the tab for mum's ongoing care. They needed to sell and they needed the plans to do it. They didn't know how so I helped them. It was a small but genuine gesture on my part but, of course, I was aware of the potential upside in building my credibility with the family in distress, and establishing a stronger relationship with them as a result. I did want to flip the house.

The second problem with the house became obvious once you stepped inside; it was full of cracks. They were widespread and severe, and without further detailed negotiation they would make the house un-mortgageable. The cracks had put a lot of viewers off and the opportunity was now confined to cash buyers only. We had a good look at the house and examined the cracks. I am no crack expert and I have no formal building qualifications but I have traded quite a few houses and there are tell-tale signs that I have seen before. We looked at the house objectively, and after consideration felt that the issues in the house could be fixed.

Now let me explain my policy with regard to cracks. I split the decision on working with cracks into two. First, if the cracks have been caused by something that has been done to the house then I would look at it favourably. For instance, maybe there have been DIY disasters that have caused them; that was what my gut feeling was when I viewed the house for the first time. There were cracks in virtually every room in the house. In the upstairs front bedroom, the cracks were very severe. They were located in both side walls of the bedroom about halfway between the rear wall and the bay shaped window which was above the ground floor bay and mirrored its shape completely. There were then further cracks located all around the bay window itself.

Our brief inspection suggested the hand of the DIY enthusiast at work. First, we believed that at the ground floor level, what had originally been two separate reception rooms had, at some point been knocked together and the wall between them had been removed. We suspected very strongly that insufficient support had been put in place and so there had been movement over the years. This would lead to cracks forming. Additionally, the house had been fitted with Aluminium frame double glazed windows.

Aluminium was a cutting edge and very popular material and was used for all sorts of products during the 1970's. It is a great product and clearly valuable when used in the right context. Without doubt there were products for which it was ideally suited. However, there were definitely some instances where it was used for purposes and products which it was not suited.

An example of one such use is in golf clubs. Golf clubs with aluminium shafts were promoted heavily in the early '70's. I remember Jack Nicklaus, the No.1 golfer in the world at that time appearing on TV to advertise the new golf clubs saying how he could swing the club faster and therefore hit the ball further, longer and straighter, but I'm not sure I completely believed him. Let me explain.

My Dad was at the time a very keen golfer, enthusiastic rather than gifted, and as with most middle aged men, had quite a gentle swing speed – probably little more than half the speed of the magnificent sporting specimen that was Jack Nicklaus. However, my Dad had seen the adverts and if golf clubs with aluminium shafts were good enough for Jack then they were good enough for him also. The new shiny clubs were ordered and arrived, and my Dad was very proud of them. He had one of the very first aluminium shaft set of clubs in the town. He went out for his regular weekend game with his pals and showing off the new "Nicklaus" clubs that were going to change his game, and possibly his life.

He got as far as the 4th tee when limbering up with his new, highly prized aluminium shafted driver, as he went to strike the ball, there was an almighty "crack" and the club snapped in more than one place and wrapped itself around his neck. There was a significant amount of inward laughing from his pals accompanied externally by mock expressions of concern and words of sympathy. On the way round the course, four more clubs snapped. By now all pretence had gone and the game was punctuated by howls of laughter alternating with moments of breathless suspense while they waited to see if the next swing would break another club shaft. To be fair, the manufacturer replaced the set without any quibble, interestingly with old fashioned steel shafts this time, but for me the incident only served to reinforce the truth that aluminium, as fine a product as it is, might not be the right solution for every situation.

And so back to our aluminium frame windows. This was a standard three bed semi-detached house with bay windows at the ground floor and first floor at the front. The bays, at their heart were made of significant pieces of wood at each corner of each window. The glazing was fitted into the wooden frames. I'm not saying that these wooden sections of the bay windows were structural, but it is undeniable that they may have been providing some support to the front of the house, and were helping to keep everything safe and sound. What the owner had done was to remove the solid, chunky pieces of wood and replace them with, what I am sure at the time were very fashionable and groovy pieces of aluminium. They were thin and streamlined which was probably considered appealing at the time.

With all this DIY stuff having gone on, and probably more that we didn't even know about, some 40-years later it is fair to say that there was a bit of rock and roll going on and the house had moved which had caused the cracks in the walls. As a result of all this, the vendor couldn't sell the house and was in some financial distress.

Since the cracking had been caused by some sort of DIY disaster, no matter how long ago the problem was caused, it met my criteria for looking at it the house in spite of it.

The other cause of cracking is much more difficult to deal with, when cracks are caused by movement of the land that the house is standing on or subsidence. That is a problem that's too difficult for me to resolve and I will not get involved with properties suffering from it. I suspect that there may be more experienced property people who are reading this that may be saying to themselves "Come on David, subsidence is an opportunity! That would be no reason to walk away if there is money to be made" and they might be correct.

As a rule of thumb, and especially if you are just starting out, do not get involved in properties affected by subsidence. Yes, you can underpin and yes, you can get all the guarantees for the work, but there is always the risk that you may not have access to the lenders you want to work with because of the issue. The other factor relating to issues of subsidence, is time. It will take time to sort out and flippers do not have the time to waste. They need to find the quickest way to make the biggest amount of money with the least work and emotional involvement. That is why I suggest this as a rule to follow:

Cracks resulting from a DIY disaster I will look at it; cracks resulting from ground which is moving is too problematic for me and I will move on.

On the day of the viewing mentioned earlier, I had been offered the house at £75,000 for a cash purchase. I did my research and it appeared that previous sale prices for near-identical properties in the same Cul-de-Sac were in the region of £101,000 to £105,000 (for houses that were in good condition). This house was not in good condition but I thought that it was saveable

Conditional Offers

We decided to make an offer of £60,000, but it was a conditional offer. You have to introduce the concept of conditional offers into your property life right from the beginning of your journey. Conditional offers are great because they can get you out of trouble, and they deal with scenarios such as this.

Imagine the situation where you have made an offer and the house is taken off the market. The sale process has advanced and six weeks down the road, after more detailed analysis you decide that you may have got your figures wrong and that you want to reduce your offer. If you do this, you will tick people off and it will also undermine you with all parties involved. You may lose face with the estate agent who offered you the house and it is the sort of thing that they don't like and will not forget, meaning that you may not get offered the best deal first, next time. It will likely take you a while to repair the damage with them.

With a conditional offer you can cover all this off up-front. Conditional offers allow you to still reduce the offer if you want, whilst maintaining goodwill at the same time. Here is the script, based on what I said in relation to the previous property. You can adapt it to your situation for your purposes.

"I am going to make you an offer. I want to make it very clear that it is conditional. It is conditional upon obtaining a structural engineer's report that will tell us exactly what is wrong with the house. If we find that the amount of work required is so large that we have to re-think our offer, then we reserve the right to reduce the offer. Does everyone understand what our offer is? On that basis we make a conditional offer of £60,000".

The purpose of this is to make sure in words of one syllable that everyone understands and there is not an expectation for us to proceed at £60,000 if we don't want to.

You need to use this type of script in your business when you are making offers.

With that all settled, and the conditional offer accepted, we got on with doing our investigation. We instructed a structural engineer who went to the house and put together a report. If you have never seen a structural engineer's report, then I can tell you that they are most helpful and not in any sense similar to the surveyors report you might see for a bank valuation obtained when you buy a house with a mortgage.

The structural engineers report features three columns. The first column tells you what is wrong with a particular feature in the house. The second column tells you how to fix it. The third column tells you how much the structural engineer thinks the cost will be for the work. This is all very useful, in particular the estimate of cost because it is always very cautious. Several times over the years we have gone on to have the work prescribed by the structural engineer quoted for by local builders, and have learned a couple of useful things out. Firstly, not everything in the report needs to be done to make the house safe and lettable. Secondly, we can usually get the essential recommended works done for about half the cost quoted by the structural engineer in the report. The cost of the report in the case of this property was around £400 plus VAT.

In this particular report, the structural engineer prescribed that the roof needed replacing. That was not just the tiles but also the main structure of the roof, because of spread. This means that the roof had sunk a bit in the middle; indeed, you could see a dip in the middle of the roof from the ground. Unresolved spread will cause problems over the years but it doesn't always mean that you have to replace the structure. We had a couple of quotes done for the work required to secure the structure of the roof as it stood at that time. In other words, we decided we would secure the roof in the state it was on that day rather than fully replacing it as recommended. It would always have the dip but it wouldn't get any worse and would serve the home owner very well for decades to come. The structural engineer estimated the works that he suggested would cost £12,000. We could get the issue resolved to a serviceable standard for £3,000.

In total the structural engineer's estimate for all the works was £28,000. We thought we could fix the house for £11,000.

However, the report put together by a professional carries great weight, so without adding our thoughts we sent it over to the other side. We sent a copy to the estate agent, to the family and to Slow & Co., the solicitor. At this point we had to have a conversation with them.

"You can see the scale of the works required here. They are of a higher level that we anticipated. We have a conditional offer in place of £60,000. The works required are £28,000. Now to be fair we have already made a low offer in anticipation of the fact that serious work needs to be done so I will not reduce our offer by the full £28,000. Our new offer is a cash offer for £46,250."

Why £46,250? A couple of reasons. Firstly, looking at the report we thought that this project was an ideal flip to auction; remember, we are all about earning the highest return in the shortest amount of time with the least amount of work. At £46,250 this house would work as a flip to auction (something that I will explain in a second).

Secondly, I need to talk about the extra £250.

At this point in my property career I had started to be educated. I had heard somewhere from Mark Homer at Progressive property that it was important to make an offer which is not a round number. So I intended to offer a straight £46,000 but added on an extra £250 because Mark Homer had said so. I am now, sometime later, aware that this is not exactly what Mark actually said and I misapplied the principle but it worked fine in any event. I have carried on doing it since except that I am much more sophisticated now. Instead of a round £250 I might get very creative and come up with a really special number. Maybe I might add on something like £139.17? Who knows what number I will come next? Even my solicitor has commented to me that it is very unusual to deal with documentation that has such strange odd numbers in, but that is ok. It is part of my image with the estate agents I work with and it is part of what makes me different and special.

You need to be different and special.

The family accepted the offer and now that we had a purchase agreed at £46,250 we had to move quickly. This was going to be a flip to auction so these are the guidelines for your first flip to auction, which will enable you to make money without doing a lot of work.

The first thing you need to do is get the auction house onside. Depending on where you are based the auction company and the personnel might be different but the principles remain the same. The auction house will have a representative who will liaise with you. When you want to enter a property into the auction, they will first come to look at the property. The first time you meet they may be a little cool and professional towards you, but don't let that put you off in any way at all. You have to understand that they are accustomed to meeting all sorts of strange people who generally have all sorts of strange ideas; that will not be you. You are going to do and say the right things and I will show you how.

Talk to the representative about value, the price that you are likely to have in your head and what you think you might achieve for the house at auction. This will set the tone for your relationship with the auction house.

In this particular case I now knew that we were buying at £46,250. I knew that we had incurred costs. The project all in, with buying costs, selling costs, the structural engineer's report and everything else would stand us in around £51,000.

We asked ourselves, who was our customer? We took the view that the most likely person to buy might be either a local person who had family nearby and wanted to buy the house for another family member so that they were all very local to each other, or it might be sold to a local builder who had the skills required to bring the house up to standard. They would understand what was required to be done, and would likely regard it as their personal project for the year to make a profit at the end.

We next asked ourselves, given that those people were our likely customer how much would they pay? Well, they needed to have a profit left in the house at the end of the day and when you are doing your numbers on a project you should always leave a margin for everyone to earn money. The project will proceed more smoothly if you do that. Working backwards from the open market value, this was my thought process.

The open market value was, say £101,000. There was plenty of evidence for that. This meant that if the auction purchaser could see a completed project in the low £90,000s, then they might be interested. The total cost of the project might come in at around £20k if the purchaser took on the full roof replacement (which indeed they did – the house now has a brand new perfectly formed and level roof). So we subtracted the £20,000 from the £90,000 which left a potential customer at auction paying around £70,000. Given that our total costs were in the region of £51,000, we were going to be generating a profit which would be close to £20,000.

This illustrates what I thought might happen but I didn't share this with the auction agent for two reasons. First, because already knew what I thought might happen, I wanted to know what he thought might happen; I already knew my view, I wanted his view. Secondly, I didn't want to be like everybody else!

What almost everybody else does when they meet an auction agent on site is they start talking. They speak a lot and tell the agent what the numbers should be. Please do not do this and instead make sure that you listen more than you speak. If the agent includes the house in an auction catalogue, then they need to sell the house. To ensure a sale, the price has to be right. They will know the area, and more importantly, they will know their auction room. Take their advice.

On this occasion the auction agent shared his views with me, and spookily enough, the numbers aligned. We were agreed on the numbers, which was good. Not only was I happy with what I heard and pleased with the likely outcome, but so was the auction agent. This is why it's so important to get your numbers right. We are now aligned and working together not arguing about the values. I cannot overstate the value of this.

The next job is to agree a "guide" price. For those of you who haven't been to a property auction before, nor seen a catalogue, there are two figures that are very important; the "guide" price and the "reserve" price.

On the face of it, the guide price appears to be intended to give a prospective purchaser a rough idea of the price the property might sell for. This is not what the guide price is for, instead it is to generate interest in the lot and to do this, the guide price has to be low. If the guide price is low, you get lots of viewings and lots of downloads of the legal pack which must accompany each lot.

The reserve price is the price set by the vendor, and is the price below which they do not want to sell. If the bidding doesn't reach the reserve price, then the house will not be sold by the auctioneer. There are no rules about the relationship between the guide price and the reserve price but there are conventions about this in the industry. It is accepted that the reserve price should not be more than 10% higher than the guide price. In low value lots, such as the one in this case study, the accepted relationship is that the reserve price should not be more than £10,000 higher than the guide price.

We set our guide price at £53,000, and if you remember that our total costs were £51,000, on the face of it this looked very low. However, it allowed us to set the reserve at £63,000 without breaking the convention and the guide price of £53,000 was intended to generate a significant amount of interest in the lot, which it did. As a back stop, you should remember that if you get it wrong you are allowed to alter the guide price, and consequently also the reserve price right up to the day of the auction itself. In this way, it all becomes a mysterious game really!

Make sure you take the auction agent's advice and play the game well.

Now that you are building your relationship and credibility with the auction agent you need to ask for their help, and here's what you should request. You need to be in the right place in the auction catalogue, ideally within the first 15 lots in the auction. Why the first 15? If you have been to a property auction, you will know that at a large auction the room is packed at the beginning. After a couple of hours, the room has thinned out a bit and by the time we get to Lot 148 you could fire a cannon across the room and not hit anyone. You need your property offered when the room is full and buzzing as it will make you more money.

In the case of this property I asked the question, the agent sucked his teeth and looked slightly pained, but he didn't say "No"!

"I will speak to the office and call you back on that" he said.

I did receive the phone call, and to be honest although I wanted a place in the first 15 lots, if he had found me a place in the first 30 lots I would have been pleased. The reason is that the auction house has to earn money, and they also know that the busiest time in the auction is during the first 30 lots. If they place your property in the first 30 lots, that means they think that it will sell and they think it will go for reasonable money. This is useful feedback for you and me that we've got it right. Their vote of confidence is what we need to confirm our expectations for the sale.

In the event, when I answered the phone, the agent told me

"We've allocated you a catalogue number... it's number 14".

"Oooooooooooh" I thought; we just slipped under the wire.

The next thing you need to do is to buy the house. The auction house cannot market the house or put it in the catalogue until you have at least exchanged contracts on the purchase, so I would only have the briefest of preliminary conversations with the auction house until you are really confident that the exchange will proceed. Once you have exchanged, then you can push on quickly because you then have a legal interest in the property and you are extremely likely to be able to complete on the purchase in most circumstances. The auction house will market the house once you have exchanged but they cannot sell it on the auction day if you have not completed.

This gives you a great opportunity for a really efficient use of money. When you exchange then, usually, you have to put down 10% of the purchase price. In the example above this was £4,625, not a huge sum. Technically you could arrange to complete the transaction on the day before the auction and in this example you would only have to produce the balance of the purchase price, plus all the costs if the sale, around £42,500, just 24 hours before the auction. To be fair, this might be cutting it a bit fine. I believe that we arranged to complete a week before the auction to allow us a margin of error. On this occasion we were using our cash to complete the deal so we had no concerns that the finance might let us down at the last moment. If you are working with joint venture finance, bridging loans or other peoples' money, then you can see how you might limit the cost of this finance by using this particular strategy.

The next job you have is to monitor the viewings and the legal packs. The legal pack is put together by your solicitor, and in the case of this particular property, it was a very efficient process. Do not forget, we do not quite own the house yet. We are going through the purchase but every legal process and document can be used simultaneously, not only to facilitate the purchase but also to populate the legal pack for the auction sale. Even a copy of the structural engineer's report goes into the legal pack, since total transparency during the process is required.

In this example there were group viewings arranged and I phoned the admin team at the auction house a few times to see what was going on. They were very efficient, and they told me that we had-had 28 viewings and 23 legal packs had been downloaded.

This was good news. I was very pleased about this because what it told me was that we had generated a lot of interest and that it was very likely that we would have a genuine auction in the room.

Now, what if the admin team had told me that we had-had only one viewing and no legal packs had been downloaded? I would have had to withdraw the property from the auction and if there was no interest then I would have had to re-think.

My fall back strategy on this property was always to do the work myself and then re-market at a retail level through the estate agent who had introduced the house to me. This is definitely a reserve strategy because it would have taken much longer and would have been significantly more expensive. This was, in effect defaulting to the Buy, Refurb and Sell model which was not really my first choice. The profit may well have been similar but I would have been tied into what would have been, in effect, a 12-month project. I may also have found that I was losing out on other opportunities along the way.

If I had wanted to get out of going through with the auction, how would I get out? You have to have withdrawal options and these will be defined in the contract that you sign with the auction house. The difficulty is, that the auction house will make it quite expensive for you to exercise this option and I have typically seen auction contracts where the cost of a late withdrawal could be as much as £2,000 plus VAT. You do not really want to pay that much. What I do, is deal with this earlier in the process when I am speaking to the auction house agent about putting the property in the auction in the first place. You will recall that I spoke to him about the catalogue position, and at the same time I spoke to him about the withdrawal option. The conversation went like this.

"If we get it wrong and we don't get enough interest then I will have to withdraw the house for the auction and try something else. Now it is only fair and reasonable that I should pay you something at that point. You will have done some administrative work, you will have printed the catalogue and probably done some viewings, but I can't afford to pay you £2,000 plus VAT to pull out of the auction. I think we need to amend that figure to £500 plus VAT at a maximum."

I got the normal, tooth sucking, *"I will have to speak to the office response"* but we left the conversation there. In this instance, when the contract came through I noted that the £2,000 fee was still in place. We never discussed it again but all I did was alter the figure in the contract to £500 with a pen and initial it. I have no idea if this would have been sufficient, because in the event the auction went ahead and I didn't need to withdraw the property. I will leave this with you to take a view on what the outcome might have been.

Chapter Nineteen: Funding The Deal

We've now reached the point in the book where we need to discuss the difficult issue of money, and it is time to be honest here; if you are going to buy houses then you will need some money. There is no way around this thorny issue so I am going to tackle it head-on. If you have cash, or access to cash then this will be easy for you. Maybe you have come into some money or you have tucked away funds over the years, which is all good. What if you don't have any money? Fortunately, if this is the case for you then it doesn't mean you can't proceed; although you need money it doesn't have to be *your* money.

Bank Of Mum And Dad

In my experience there are three common ways of raising money. The most popular and common today is the Bank of Mum and Dad. The Baby Boom generation, of which I am a member is the wealthiest generational group that has ever existed. They were born after the Second World War when there was a baby boom to celebrate the end of hostilities and the return to normality. The era of Baby Boomers went on for nearly 20 years and is commonly viewed as continuing until 1964. I am part of that group.

As a group we lived at an extraordinary time and were the recipients of an extraordinary amount of support in the form of full employment, government subsidies, education and asset growth. I see all around me on a daily basis, members of the Baby Boomer generation supporting their children or grandchildren on their journey through life. People born during that post war period understand that things have changed and it is harder if you are starting out today. What I am saying, is go and see your Mum and Dad and see if they will help you on your way. You might be surprised!

On the other hand, you might say to me *"No that is not going to work for me so how else can I do this?"* Well, let's think this through. Maybe you have benefited from capital growth in your lifetime? I meet many friends who are new to property and who say to me "Look we've built up a bit of equity in our home over the last few years. If we took £50,000 out would that get us started?"

Absolutely that would get them started! It might not get them started inside the M25, but in certain areas of the UK it would work really well, either on its own or as a deposit to which they could add a Buy-to-Let mortgage which they could then use to purchase an investment property to keep.

You can't use a Buy-to-Let mortgage (BTL) if you are buying a property to flip, the reason being that a Buy-to-Let mortgage is designed as a long term loan. It is designed to help you over a long period, typically 25 years, and of course it is designed for the lender to earn interest over a 25-year period too. If you intend to flip, then you need the money for a much shorter period, maybe nine to twelve months. If you set up a BTL mortgage with the intention of paying it back in under a year, and tell this to the bank, they will not lend. If you set it up and don't tell the bank but just pay the money back after a short period of time then you might get away with it once, but if you intend to grow a business of flipping and keep doing it, then BTL lenders will spot the pattern and they will become upset. This could affect your mortgageablity and could become an inconvenience as you grow. For your flipping business, if you don't quite have enough money then there are other avenues open to you.

The two main options, are joint venture finance or bridging.

Joint Venture Finance

Joint venture finance is probably the most popular option. This involves working with someone who has the money but doesn't have your drive or knowledge to make money from a flip. Typically, they will finance the deal but you will do all the work, and you split the profits. This can work really well when you are starting out and once you have done a few joint venture deals then you will have built up your own funds so you can do this on your own.

Finding Joint Venture finance partners is about building your credibility, first as a person and then, later as a property person. In order to explain what I mean by that, consider the situation. If you had funds and were looking to get into property but had no time, who would you want to work with? Ideally, it would be someone who has property experience, but what if you stepped up to them, with the right knowledge, the right strategy, as someone who is honest, principled, hardworking, enthusiastic, determined and an attractive person to work with. Do you think that someone might want to work with you? They will... I am telling you they will. Not everyone will want to of course, but there are enough people out there with money who are looking for people like you – a person exactly like you. They are looking for someone with a plan, with drive and ambition, who wants to improve their life, someone who is honest and trustworthy and just needs a helping hand to get on their way. They will be especially interested if you are offering half the profits in return for their cash investment. I encourage you to go and put yourself out there. Go to your property network meeting and start growing your list of potential people you will want to work with. When you go to your breakfast meeting, tell everyone what you do. If you persist in doing this, then it will work and people will come to you with finance.

The reason why this works is all to do with the state of the economy and the amount of interest that investors are getting on their money while it's invested in the bank. Savers today are in effect receiving a negative interest rate on their savings. The actual interest rate received from the banks is tiny and is significantly less than the inflation that we are suffering in the economy at this time. In addition to this there are still trust issues with respect to the banks. At the moment, savers money is protected only up to a maximum of £85,000. In Europe, that is 100,000 euros. Savers have not forgotten the very recent past experiences, where banks in Europe have betrayed savers' trust on more than one occasion. In 2012 and 2013 banks in Europe most notably in Cyprus, in effect nationalised savings that were held in Cypriot banks, and every penny over 100,000 euros was lost by the saver. For reasons such as this, people are flocking to property as a safer investment for their funds. The advantages of property are obvious since immediately the investor places their money into property they are investing in a bricks and mortar asset which, over time will appreciate in value. The inflationary pressure on their money that was being eaten away on a daily basis is halted. At the same time the return on their money, now based on either holding a property where the rent-roll is managed on a monthly basis, or if flipping a house, is invested in a project that in the short term should produce at least a 20% return on investment, is far more secure.

There are rules and regulations concerning the marketing of your projects and trying to attract joint venture finance. If I really went into the detail here, then I could write a small book just on the regulations that have to be applied to joint ventures. If you want the real heavyweight detail, then go and look it up. Joint ventures are regulated by the FCA.

What you need to know is that in law there are two different types of investor. These investors are known as Sophisticated Investors and Non-Sophisticated Investors. Sophisticated investors are people with a significant income and cash assets. They have a track record and history in business or in investment that shows that they are competent to make their own decisions on investment opportunities.

Non-sophisticated investors are people who cannot show that track record and history and who do not have the large funds as laid down by the regulations. If you have any concerns as to whether you are breaching regulations, then there is a very simple way to deal with this. If you borrow money from somebody based on an interest rate return over a fixed period, then you will not be breaching any regulation.

If you are working with an investor based on a profit split on the deal, then you have to be more careful. Do not forget that the regulations are not about doing joint ventures, instead they are about advertising joint ventures. If you are speaking to a family member, or somebody that you've known for many years, you can on a one-to-one basis, agree a joint venture with them based on a profit split. That is entirely legal and within the regulations.

If you are working with a joint venture partner, then there will be a cost to your arrangement. Normally there will be a profit split on the deal, which is normally 50/50, but that is not set in stone. Don't be too greedy though. You are better off doing a 50/50 split and doing a few deals with your joint venture partner than trying to keep too much profit and not getting any deals done.

WORKING WITH INVESTORS

Attracting Investors To Finance Your Flips

'In business, kid, "the Main Thing is to keep the Main Thing the Main Thing"' Stephen Covey

Now to be fair, I have never heard Stephen Covey's voice, but in my head whenever I read that sentence I always hear it being spoken in the croaking voice of a 2000-year-old man; I am not sure why. I know that Stephen Covey was not a 2000-year-old man. Perhaps it is because I am acutely aware of the wisdom within those words. I am also pretty certain that the "In business, kid..." bit of that sentence comes from within my head and not from the learned and distinguished Mr Covey. I think the 2000-year-old man just tagged it on.

For me, that sentence, Mr Covey's sentence, is the most important sentence within this book and the reason is that newcomers to property investing and flipping are so easily distracted. Do not get distracted! The point is that property investing and flipping houses can actually be very simple. However, the industry and commentators and other trainers, many of whom have not bought or flipped a deals in years, like to make it seem complicated. Additionally, newcomers to the strategy take their eye off the main things which are finding the money (maybe from the Bank of Mum and Dad, or maybe by finding joint venture investors, or maybe by working with bridging finance), and then finding a deal that stacks.

All you have to do is put the two together and get paid.

In this chapter we are going to talk about the most important thing of all the Main Things which is your exit. This is bit where the rubber hits the road, the bit in your flip where you get paid, the most important part of the process. Many times I get asked "David, what should I do first, find the deal or find the funds to help finance the deal?". The answer of course, is that to have a viable business you need both. That said, I am absolutely convinced, and the longer I do this the more convinced I become, that the most important part of this equation is to find the money first.

If you find the money first, the whole process becomes so much easier. You know what you want from the deal, you know what you are looking for in terms of margin and return whether you are working with your own funds or whether you are working with joint venture partners. Getting it then becomes a tick box exercise, you can just go shopping and it's fun.

However, what I see time and again is a bit of hesitation from friends who are new to the industry with respect to marketing themselves to potential joint venture partners and who delay in meeting with the people who have money. This is really understandable because they are new to looking for deals and going through the process and they think that they might mess up and let people down, especially people who have trusted them with their money. Because they are new, they tend not to be confident that they are in a position to serve a joint venture partner. They find the prospect of one-to-one conversations with anyone who might have money a bit daunting because they are concerned that the person with the cash might know more than they do. They are worried that their inexperience will cost them, and the potential partner might choose to work with someone else.

Time and again, this is what I see. Instead of marketing themselves to joint venture partners first, our new Flipper will decide to start trawling the online resources looking for a "deal" and this is where things start to go wrong on day one. What exactly are they looking for? How do they know if they have found a potential purchase or a flip when they don't know if they have the money to buy it in the first place? If they do find something that they think might be a deal, what are they going to do with it?

Often, at the start of their journey they don't have the confidence to go out at the start finding investors so they retreat into their laptops and start scraping the online portals, Rightmove, Zoopla and others hoping to find the "deal". The thing is they don't have the money in place to move the "deal" forward even if they do find it, which they knew when they started looking. They can spend maybe 100 hours online looking for a "deal" and then they find a "deal" but they can't do anything with it because they haven't got an investor so they have to let it go again.

It is wasteful. It is demoralising. Don't do it.

I am going to make this very easy for you and suggest that you start by finding your investor. Don't worry, I am going to show you how to do this and there are many ways that you can do it. I'm going to share with you what has worked for me, and if you do what I have done then it will work for you too.

There are two main ways to find investors; face-to-face and online which both work. They have both worked for me and they continue to work. I'm going to give you the blueprint that I use to find investors to buy my deals.

Face-To-Face Meetings

Let's start with face-to-face. Where can you meet potential property investors who might buy your deals? The answer is everywhere. Everyone you know, everyone you meet is a potential customer for your flip or a client for your Deal Packaging business. Never assume that they aren't interested; rule number one is tell everyone you know and everyone you meet, what you do.

You can use what I was taught as the "Three-foot rule". The way this works, is that you tell everyone who comes within three feet of you what you do. Try doing it all day, every day for seven days. Don't miss any opportunity. It is important.

Initially you may feel uncomfortable but this will soon pass and by the end of the seven days, all the discomfort will have passed. Not everyone will be interested in your new business but that is okay. The purpose of the exercise is for you to become comfortable with what you do. At the same time, it puts you in danger of finding an investor for your new property business, so don't be surprised if somebody that you talk to actually shows an interest and wants to know more. To be clear, you have to do it for seven days. Don't do it for two and a half days and then give up because in your head you have a little voice saying "These people don't want to know what you are doing. Please stop embarrassing me by telling them". You have to do it for a full seven days and you will then have lost the little voice. It will have faded away and you will have no issues talking to anyone about what you do going forward.

The next question is what do you say to them? You need to prepare what is known as an "elevator pitch", so named because it should allow you to express exactly what it is that you do in the amount of time it takes for an elevator (or as we say in English, a lift) to complete its journey. If you find yourself trapped in a lift with a stranger, then make sure you practice your elevator pitch to them in the ten or so seconds before they reach their floor.

To help you on your way, I'm happy to share my elevator pitch which has been honed and refined over years of speaking it out loud. In the early days I would genuinely practice it in the bathroom mirror whilst having a shave. Today it goes something like this:

"What I do is increase the wealth of my investors".

That's it. That is all I say. Then nine times out of ten the person I am speaking to will ask to know more. *"Oh, how do you do that exactly?"* Then I can tell them, in detail. You can use my elevator pitch if you like it, or you can make one of your own. The important thing is to make sure you have one. Make sure you have a concise form of words that explains exactly what you do in just a few seconds and make sure you practice it.

I'll confess, that this was not my first elevator pitch, and my early elevator pitches were not good. I remember that the breakthrough came when I was having a session with my property mentor at the time and he asked:

"Do you have an elevator pitch?"

"Absolutely", I replied.

"Well let's hear it then"

And it went something like this.

"My name is David Siegler. I source properties in the North West of England for investors who are based in the South East of England. We get great BMV, with exceptional ROI and we try to get a really big ROCE"

"No, that's rubbish" my mentor shared with me

"Why is it rubbish? That's what everyone else says?"

"Well exactly. You have to be different. You want to grab people's attention so they know you are different. You need to work on that".

I really took his advice to heart, and for the next few months I tried. My local property network meeting in Brighton is the Property Investors Network (PIN) meeting. It was the only property network meeting in the town at the time and in fact, it is still the only property network meeting in the town. It is a great meeting with a room of 70-80 property people meeting every month, run by a great host, the wonderful Peter Fannon. The thing about PIN meetings is that they have something called the "20 second Service Provider" slot.

Just before the coffee break in the middle of the evening, everyone in the room gets the opportunity to stand in front of the room and can explain what they do, and it is free to do so. Now of course, not all the delegates stand up but quite a few do, and I joined in. I remembered the advice that my mentor had given me and I tried to be different.

I may have gone too far.

I cannot remember the content of all the slots I contributed, but I know that they were not specifically about property. They became more about commenting on topical events of the day. For instance, I recall very well that one of the Brighton PIN events coincided with the day that Jason Orange announced that he had left Take That. In my 20 second Service Provider slot that day I remember that I shared with the room how sad I was that Jason Orange had left Take That because nobody cared. Not even Take That cared. They just carried on as a trio as if nothing had changed.

"Now I remember the day when Robbie Williams left Take That. It was like a day of national mourning. Young women were weeping openly in the streets. I felt a bit emotional myself."

Having shared my thoughts, I just sat down again.

The effect of this change of approach was quite interesting. About six months into this change of approach, the room was actually looking forward to hearing what I had to say. I had become this strange character who, in his strangeness, was contributing something unique to the evening. Delegates were actually waiting to hear what I was going to say each month. It was all a bit of fun really and that is the point. We were enjoying it. To be fair, our host Peter Fannon was very patient with me. He gave me enough time to say what I was trying to say.

When the time came for me to switch to a pitch about a property, the result was that I sold a pub in Oldham during the 20 Second Service Provider slot at Brighton PIN. I had been quite strategic about it, and when the host invited people to share, quite a few hands would go up. I wanted to go last and while there is no science to this, there always seemed to be a moment when the hand raises would slow and thin out. That was when I decided to join in. I'm not quite sure if I did actually go last on that night, but here is what I said:

"I'm really embarrassed. I've bought a pub in Oldham. It cost me £80,000. It is very ugly. I don't know why I did it."

"On the other hand I spoke to the Planning Department in Oldham and they say that I can turn it into 10 bed HMO. But that will cost another £80,000..."

"But on the other hand we have a pre-agreed valuation with a commercial lender who said that when it is completed it will have a value of just over £400,000 which means that we can draw down just under £300,000."

"If you would like to speak to me about this then I will be standing next to the flower pot during the break."

I went to the flower pot and waited to see what happened and one man came over. Just one, but that was enough. That man didn't buy it but as a direct result of that conversation we sold the pub in Oldham and earned a £15,000 fee. This stuff works.

The next piece of equipment that you need is a business card. You will see on the property forums all sorts of accepted wisdom about business cards and I have collected thousands of them over the years, featuring some pretty weird and wonderful designs. You will receive advice that says you need your details on the front of your card together with your photo so the person who collects your card won't forget what you look like, and that you need your company logo on the reverse of the card. I take a slightly different view in that I don't believe any of that advice is worthwhile. In fact, for the last three years I haven't used a business card at all. When I meet someone that I want to connect with then I just ask them to exchange text messages with me there and then, so that we have each other's phone numbers in our phone books. Now that might be a bit too far for some of the purists out there, especially for those of you who are looking to build an email database of investors for the future, so I have had a rethink.

I now have a brand new business card which is printed on plain white card in an ordinary finish, no fancy textures, nothing shiny, and on the front it just has my name, my phone number and my email address. It is in a very conservative, understated print and nothing too flamboyant. On the reverse of the card it is just plain white. The reason I keep it plain on the back is that if I meet a person that I want to meet up with again and they don't have a business card of their own then I can write their details on the back of one of my cards and keep hold of it. My business card is a practical piece of equipment that is designed to do a particular job, that being to pass on my contact details and to gather the contact details of others. Play around with different templates, colours and layouts for business cards by all means since a lot of this is down to personal taste. Just make sure the card does the job it is supposed to do and that it is to be used as a practical piece of equipment that will help you in your business.

Now we are feeling a bit more comfortable about what we do. We have our business cards in our hand, and we have our elevator pitch honed and practiced and ready to be launched like an Exocet missile. Where should we go? Well objective number one, top of the list has to be Property Network Meetings. That is where you will meet likeminded people who will listen to you and may show interest in what you do. There are various types of network meeting, such as the fabulous meetings run by Progressive Property Network. Another large provider is the PIN group, and there are many network meetings which are independent and do their own thing. Where can you find a list of all the network meetings in existence so that you can plan your assault on the unsuspecting property fraternity? Well very thoughtfully, our friends at YPN magazine include a full list of all the property network meetings at the back of every edition that they produce. I suggest that you subscribe, get hold of your magazine and have a look. Alternatively, you can borrow a recent edition from a friend who does subscribe and read theirs; that will work too.

Once you have spotted a couple of network meetings near to where you live, or near to where you hope to market your flips then you are all set to attend. The most important rule of network meetings is that you have to go to them. When I say you have to go, I don't mean that you have to go once but rather that you have to commit to going regularly. You have to become a part of that community of property people and you have to go through the "know, like and trust" process that all human beings have to go through when they are building relationships in property, in business and, well, in life really. Make sure you go to every meeting. Become part of the room and become someone that everyone else expects to see when they attend that event. It doesn't happen in the first few visits but over a period of five or six months you should be able to establish yourself as one of the key members of that community. At Progressive Property Network (PPN) events there is a bit of a short cut for this since you can ask your host if you may become a founder member, which is a big opportunity for you.

Being a founder member at a PPN meeting will really help you to build your profile since it elevates you from being one of the 50 or so other delegates in the room. You are different and you are one of the "in" crowd. You get to hang out with the cool kids in the team, and you get close to your PPN host which is vital to do. The PPN host at any meeting is at the centre of a web which includes every contact for any service that you might ever possibly want at any point in your power team. If you are looking to package deals, then you will need a local power team to serve your investors. You will need property solicitors, accountants, mortgage brokers, commercial mortgage brokers, bridging finance providers, insurance brokers, lettings professionals, contractors for small jobs, contractors for big jobs and anything else that you might ever need in the running of a property business. Your PPN host knows who these people are and they will give you access to all of them. Get close to your PPN host.

Another bonus of being a founder member at a PPN meeting is that every month you are introduced to the room and you are invited to share with the room exactly what service you provide, which is very valuable. One of the best ways of getting your message out there is to speak at the front of any room and to tell people what you do. People will listen and when they are ready people will come. You have to get your voice heard and tell everyone what you do.

Once you have found your favourite property network meeting, you've started to build yourself a bit of a profile, what do you do next? Well, you go and network. That is what it is all about! You must get out there and meet people.

I am constantly puzzled by network meetings and the delegates that attend them. Most network meetings start at 7pm. Ideally you should get there early, around 6.30pm so you can network. I am honoured to be the current Host of the Mayfair PPN network meeting and this is what I observe.

Most delegates don't arrive early to network, but instead arrive at 6.58 pm so that they don't *have* to network. That is why most network meetings begin late because most of the delegates arrive at 2 minutes to 7.00pm and it takes a few minutes to get them through registration. There is usually a break during the evening for networking at which point most delegates run to the loo, or stay very close to the people they know or came along with. Some might stand at the back or to one side of the room, pretending that they have to deal with a very important text. They haven't got to deal with a very important text, they are just trying to avoid speaking to anyone so they don't have to network. At the end of the evening there is always the opportunity to meet in the bar for more networking, but most delegates disappear quickly and run home so that they don't have to take part. Why do they call them network meetings if nobody wants to network?

That is certainly not how we are going to do it. Instead, we are going to put ourselves out there and we are going to network. You've got your card and your elevator pitch, so step up and step out and meet someone new. Remember, the object of the exercise in my view is to cover as much ground as you possibly can and meet people that you can work with. The object has to be to collect eight to ten business cards from people in the room, and collecting the card is not enough on its own; they have to be qualified cards.

By qualified, I mean that you have approached someone, made eye contact, shaken them by the hand and you have exchanged business cards. The trick now is not to get stuck in a long and drawn-out conversation. The only verbal exchange that is compulsory is as follows:

"Thank you so much for your card. Is it okay if I call you in the next couple of days to fix a meeting to see if we have any common ground?"

This sentence is really important and what you have done is told them that you are going to call. You have told them that the purpose of the call is to fix up a meeting with them. You are seeking their express permission that this will be ok.

If they say yes, then you are in. Make sure you call.

"Hi it's David here, we met at the network meeting the other night. I am really looking forward to meeting up with you. Would Tuesday lunchtime or Thursday afternoon be better?"

You have their permission to call and you have called to fix a meeting as you told them you would. You are offering a choice of times to give them an opportunity to say yes. If you offer only one date and time, it may not be convenient for them and that gives them the opportunity to say "No".

Sometimes, they might say "No" when you ask if it is okay to give them a call to fix a meeting which is fine. Maybe they aren't ready or maybe they feel they have nothing to offer you. Whatever the reason is, do not fret. Just move on to the next person. Nobody is going to agree to a meeting with you in the middle of the working day if they don't have a reason to meet. If they are breaking into their day, then you presumably have some common ground to discuss.

The purpose, your main purpose in attending the network meeting in the first place is to obtain qualified business cards. By qualified I mean cards from people who actually want to speak with you.

Here is the arithmetic, based on my numbers as they have evolved over time. I aim to get eight qualified cards per network meeting and when I ring all eight, then two of the prospects will agree to meet with me. If I can get to two network meetings a week (and in London this is quite easy), then this will provide four investor meetings each week. That will become 16 meetings with potential investors in a month. If I meet with 16 potential investors in a month then between two and four will be prepared to work with me and have funds available. If you find two to four new, highly qualified investors per month then you have a business my friend, and you can go shopping for flips and start making money. That is the truth of it, but people don't do it.

Why don't they all do it?

Using this one strategy you will have enough business to keep you going for a year. Why aren't you doing it?

The next job you need to do is to get yourself a portfolio. This is one of the best tips I have ever had to help me in my property business and it came from a post in the Progressive Community Facebook Group by Rob Moore. He repeats the tip occasionally so you may see it yourself going forward. My "folio" has earned me thousands of pounds' worth of business.

What Rob suggested is that we all get ourselves a really smart, leather-bound, display portfolio, which might cost around £35 on Amazon. Inside the cover there are a number of clear plastic sleeves, and into every sleeve we can insert the details of a deal or a property that we have sold. We might include the Estate Agents particulars, the floorplans, a quotation by a builder for any works, a print out of room rents locally or comparable rental for similar properties. In fact, the portfolio should contain anything that you would need to work out if it would be a great deal or not, and it should all be put it into that same clear plastic sleeve. You use one sleeve per deal.

I went on to Amazon and invested in my "folio". To be fair, I did skimp a little and went for the plastic option at £12.99 but it worked just the same. It was brilliant! Before long I had 30 or 40 sleeves in my portfolio filled with flips and deals that I had done and I only included flips and deals that were complete in my portfolio. I didn't include projects that were for sale and never sold anything from my portfolio.

The power of flicking through page after page of completed deal particulars in front of an investor is extraordinary. Your credibility soars and your authority is transformed. Whatever the investor is looking for, then you become "it". The fact that so many investors have trusted you and backed you with their money and their faith is utterly compelling. You grab the potential investor's attention and it helps you sell your service and your next deal.

Now, I know what some of you are thinking.

"That is alright for you David. You have done some deals. You have stuff to put into your portfolio. But what about me? I am just starting out and I haven't done a deal yet. What can I put into my portfolio?"

That is a fair question, and here is what I would suggest in response. If you are right at the start, there are still things you can put into your portfolio to give you credibility. Put in information about yourself. You may not have experience in property but you will likely have great experience in other aspects of life. You may have achieved some extraordinary things and if so, put a reference about them into your folio. Instead of deals that you have sold, put in a few examples of the type of deals that you will be sourcing in your area. You will have chosen your area and your strategy to add value for your investors, so go to Rightmove and pull of a few representative examples of the type of properties you think you will be marketing and the calculations which will show the potential investors what the profit might be.

Before long, your portfolio will start to include some completed deals as well. Fantastic job - you are on your way.

Recommendations And Referrals

This is a really important source of new clients for your property business but it is sometimes overlooked which is a shame, as it is a gift for you. If you have been working with an investor and done a really good job then your relationship with them will be very strong at this point. It is easy for them to have the confidence in you to speak to one or two of their contacts for the purposes of recommending and referring you, and you should always ask them if they'd be willing to do so. It is a really efficient way to find new prospects for your investor list and you absolutely need to nail the script on this.

"Thank you for spending time with me today. Now that you know what I do is there anyone you know who might benefit from having a coffee with me?"

Don't only use this when you talking to investors that you have worked with. Remember when you have the meetings with the eight prospects that you met through networking, only two of them might work with you going forward. Make sure you ask the other six for a referral or two as well. In this circumstance, although they don't know you as well as the investors who have worked with you, you do have an advantage in that they might be feeling slightly embarrassed that they have taken up your time but no business has been done. Make sure you ask them for referral also, and don't leave any meeting empty handed. At the end of the year all of these leads will add up.

Finding Investors Online

Today, the easiest way of attracting investors to you is by showing what you do online. It is a well -established route to building your brand as someone who is trustworthy, responsible and professional. I have done it, and the people that you know and love in property have done it too. There is no reason why you shouldn't do it too, and the big bonus is that it's free!

In terms of where you should start building your brand, every social media source is ripe for you to develop a profile that shares who you are and what you do. You can present yourself on Facebook. LinkedIn, YouTube, Instagram or whatever. The issue is that this world is forever changing and what might be the best advice today as to where to start building your brand could change over time. Algorithms can change and fashions can change, but these changes apply only to the platforms where you might try to build your profile. With respect to *how* you promote yourself, there are fundamentals that will never change so what I propose is to share with you what I have done and what I have tried. You will then have a template upon which to build your brand, whichever strand of social media is in fashion at the time and whichever you decide to use.

At the time of writing, Facebook is still the number one resource for building your brand to position yourself to investors. I am experimenting with LinkedIn, as apparently that has had a lot of attention recently and the algorithms on Facebook have changed making access to your audience more difficult to secure. LinkedIn at this moment is the "new" Facebook and I have to say that the jury is out at the present time. In my world, Facebook seems to still be a very powerful machine and I have not had a huge amount of measurable engagement on LinkedIn. For my business, Facebook still reaches out to plenty of people, more than enough for me and my purposes.

I am also at this time experimenting with YouTube and Instagram. Both platforms have altered the way that they present themselves to consumers and it may well be that they become pivotal to reaching out to property people in the future. For the moment, Facebook is still the number one social media asset in my locker.

Once you've joined Facebook and you have a profile, what do you do next? If you are building a brand on Facebook, then the first thing you need to do is set up a page as well as your private profile. This is a book regarding property, not social media, but there are a few essential things you need to know and grasp to make a success of this, and success in this context means appealing to property investors.

You need a Facebook page, which is in addition to your profile and there are various advantages to this. The first and most obvious is that you can separate the content to serve you best depending on which you are updating and using. You are able to keep your personal friends and family completely separate from your business contacts which has advantages. First of all, your friends and family don't have to sit through your property business posts and of course, your potential investors and business partners will not have to endure posts about your holidays; you know the ones when you take a picture of your feet on a sunbed and post it for the world to see, or maybe a picture of your dinner. This is a positive for both sides.

Having a Facebook page gives you much more opportunity to boost your business profile and reach more people, as you can advertise on Facebook and experiment as to who can see your posts. If you have identified that your key demographic is a certain age of person, living in a certain type of property, with a significant, high income, and also in certain professions or job backgrounds with particular spending habits then your Facebook page will allow you to get your message out to those particular people. This is very valuable, but be careful about the amount of money you commit to your promotions. If you commit a particular sum of money to an advertising campaign, then Facebook will certainly spend it for you and you will not receive any change. Take care in managing your budgets.

You should also study the data and analytics which Facebook provides for you. The great beauty of having a Facebook page is that you can track engagement with your posts. You can see how many people are looking at you posts and if, for example it is a video post then you will be able to see exactly how deeply people are engaging with it as opposed to just flicking through and skating over it. This is very valuable feedback for you.

The first thing to establish via your social media presence is to describe why investors might want to work with you, and why are you different from the rest. The key to this is in giving valuable and useful content. You should post as much content as you possibly can to build their trust in you and to demonstrate that you know your stuff.

What can you do for people? Can you help investors achieve their financial goals? Can you help vendors move on from their troubled situation? It all has to be a win-win.

"You can have everything in life that you want if you will just help enough other people get what they want" -Zig Ziglar

Be that person. In terms of property, become the go-to person that your investor needs in order to build their portfolio and become financially stronger. If you build that win-win then you will be handsomely paid for doing it.

Using your social media presence, talk about your story whether it is in property or, if you are new, in other aspects of life. If you are new to property and packaging you may think that this is harder, but it really isn't. People want to hear your story, to understand what were you doing before, and how you came into property?

Your message is your brand, which is who you are; let your message shine through.

How you get started depends how confident you are and how familiar you are with the process of using social media. For a start you can just join the existing conversations by going onto Facebook and commenting and supporting others who are on the journey. You should make positive comments such as "Well-done you", "What a lovely project". Your goal in engaging should be to post anything that means that your face starts to be seen and in a positive way that boosts your profile with the community. Try to contribute and add value, and if someone is asking for help and you are in a position to assist them then make sure you get out there and spread your word. If you have experience in situations that someone else is struggling with, it gives you the opportunity to establish yourself as someone who can help and who is supportive.

As a word of warning, I suggest that you don't jump in to a thread where you have no experience and cannot assist. It will not help you in your cause and if someone questions your advice within the thread, then you may have to backtrack which may undermine your standing a little within the community. It is easy to do and I have done it. My advice came from a good place but I didn't have complete command of the issues at hand and then it went a little bit wrong. Don't worry too much though, as this stuff is a little bit like yesterday's fish and chip paper; it soon gets forgotten.

Another key question regarding Facebook groups and forums, is where do you start? I would recommend looking very carefully at the property groups and forums on Facebook as some of them and very good and supportive, and others less-so. Below is a strategy that you might want to consider.

Search property groups via your Facebook profile page and join half a dozen. Follow them over a period of a few weeks to see if you feel comfortable there and if they are your sort of people. If you are happy stay in the group, stay, but if you aren't comfortable in the group then just leave. Then find a few new groups and go through the process again. In due course you will find two or three groups where you feel happiest. That is what happened to me and via experimentation I have found my favourite groups where I post all of my contributions. This strategy will work for you too.

When selecting Facebook groups to join, remember that size *does* matter. You need a critical mass in the group to make your voice heard and there are both large and small groups out there. A good, big group is what you need. By big, I mean around 20,000 members. That is a sensible number and more than enough to get your voice heard. If you can get established in two or three of those, then even where there are overlaps where individuals are members of multiple groups, there are still more than enough people to hear you story and to buy your deals.

Once you've got your page, sourced your groups and started to contribute, now you are ready to start creating our own content. Start on your Facebook page and if you are creating video content then you can store this on your YouTube channel.

I suggest that you start by building little micro blogs about what your plans are. Talk about your geography, why an investor would want to invest there and so-on. You might also discuss what infrastructure plans exist as maybe there are transport or major new employment projects in the pipeline. This type of thing will result in forced growth in property prices and explain why people should come to you to invest.

Video is a great tool for selling your services and if you are brave enough then I cannot recommend its use more highly. I understand that at the beginning it may be a little daunting, but the answer as in most things in life is to practice. Start out by familiarizing yourself with your equipment for this. Your smartphone is good enough in terms of quality to do a great job. You should video yourself in the privacy of your own office or home and you learn so much once you start doing it. I was told off by my wife the other day because I launched myself into the delights of a particular Facebook live video and I was so excited to get my story out there that I had absentmindedly left my office door open. Why would this matter? Well, what you won't be aware of is that my office is located in the extension at our home and the rest of the extension houses our utility area. By leaving the door open my viewers could see into the inner-sanctum of our utility area and a very good friend of mine told me that she did enjoy the Facebook live but she was distracted for much of the content by the sight of my underpants drying on the airer, just outside my office but in full view of the audience over my left shoulder! You need to pay attention to this stuff. If the video had been recorded, hopefully I would have noticed the gaff and pushed the door closed for the re-take.

Live broadcasts may sound a bit daunting for you at this stage and that is all good. Don't worry about it for now, but keep doing recorded videos on your phone. Keep the good ones and delete the ones that you don't like, whether that's because you have pants over your shoulder of for some other reason. You can then upload them onto your Facebook page and from there you can share them into your chosen favourite groups. You can also upload them onto your YouTube channel where you will start to build a library of content that anyone coming along in future, maybe when they discover you a year or two later can binge watch as if they have discovered a really entertaining box-set that they missed first time around.

Content is always an issue for the new property person who is set on their way to build a profile. "What shall I write Dave? What shall I say?" There is no end to the content you can share and at every point there is loads of stuff that property people will enjoy and want to see.

The first thing you can do is diarize your journey. It doesn't matter where in the journey you are, there is always interest in this. If you are just starting out, then take a picture on your phone of yourself outside an estate agents office. The mini-blog might go something like this:

"Hi all. I'm just stepping into this estate agent to see what they have and to practice my scripts with the agents so that my presentation improves. I will let you know how I get on."

Then you have to let them know how you get on; it's important to do what you have said you will do.

"Well that was a really great meeting. I was welcomed by the estate agent and they understood exactly what I am doing and what I am looking for. It seems they are human after all!" People will love this stuff.

Other posts I have seen that have worked, are when friends are just starting out on a direct mail campaign. They will take a photo of themselves, maybe standing by a letter box with a handful of addressed and stamped envelopes ready to go. This shows that the property friend is active, busy and out there working away trying to find deals and further their business, which is all good. Mix it up and property friends will love it.

You can talk in posts and videos about the viewings that you do. Take a photo of yourself outside a house that you are about to view.

"I'm just going in to have a look around, I've just seen the estate agent pull up outside in the car".

After the viewing, add a comment to the thread saying what you saw. Add photos of anything that looks a bit strange or which might make you uncertain. People love looking at photos of cracks! Find a picture of a crack and you will get all sorts of people chipping in with advice, and the great thing is that every time a friend chips in with a comment on the thread then your post will go back to the top of the forum threads again. Another very popular way to build engagement in a post such as this, is to take a picture of a plant in the back garden, and comment something like:

"Hi, I've just done a viewing of a house and found this plant in the back garden. Does this look like Japanese Knotweed to you?"

The comments will keep coming, as property forum people love giving their 10 cents worth on Japanese Knotweed, what it is, what it looks like, how to get rid of it and so-on. You will get engagement on this type of thread for days.

It is a very tactical point and you need to ensure that you get visibility for your posts. You need them to be at the top of the threads. If several friends comment with help or good advice, then it gives you the opportunity to comment again, individually obviously on each of the further comments so that you go back to the top again. Using this tactic, I have on occasion been able to maintain a post near or around the top of a forum for the best part of a week. That is a very valuable asset in a forum where there are some 20 thousand members because in a forum of that size a post can sink very quickly where so many other friends can, and do contribute.

Remember in diarizing your journey what we are trying to do is to build engagement in your chosen forum and to get people to interact with you. It is a fantastic tool that not enough friends utilize sufficiently and you need to get on it.

In terms of other ways in which you can build your credibility and put yourself out there to build your brand on social media, well why not try interviews? Video an interview on your phone with someone who has credibility in the industry and this will result in great content for those listening or watching. When deciding who to interview, it should preferably be someone who is a couple of steps ahead of you on their journey and who can share some insight. It should be someone that other property people who are just starting out like you, might like to see. Make sure you seed the fact that you are going to publish the interview ahead of time on your social media and pick a specific time when you are going to publish. Then let everybody know to expect it and build anticipation. I find that a Sunday evening at around 8.00pm is a great time to put this type of video out and again you can record it in advance, or do it live.

Bridging Finance

Let's now talk about bridging finance. I am a big fan of bridging but potential borrowers do get a bit nervous about it and I think this is because they have heard stories about the history of bridging and some nightmare tales along the way; it's not like that today. It's a completely different animal, especially if you set it up correctly in the first place.

The most important thing is to find yourself a really first-class mortgage broker, as they are the ones who can guide you through the process of bridging. In my experience, brokers have got much more clued up about the power of bridging in recent years. It is much more competitive and user friendly, but you have to know who to go to for advice. I have my own favourite contacts for bridging but I can't name them in the book because if I do, they may move on or change companies or change careers and it will make the book look a little out of date. But I will say this, if any of you want to work with the people who arrange the bridging in my life then email me and I will give you the up-to-date contact details of those who I work with.

The things that friends new to the industry worry about with bridging is really high rates of interest and being stuck on a bridge at a very high interest rate and not being able to pay it back, circumstances that may lead to them losing the property. These concerns can be seriously mitigated if you set the thing up properly in the first place. In order to do this, you must work with someone who knows what they are doing.

In my experience the total cost of bridging comes in at around 20% of the profit in the flip. The cost won't be presented like that, but that is roughly what it will be. You can see that it is cheaper than going into a Joint Venture arrangement where you might need to give 50% of your profit away. In terms of risk then no bridging finance organisation today will lend you money if the exit is not assured at the outset. I know we are talking about flipping the deal here and walking away with the cash but what if, because of unforeseen issues either in your project or in the market as a whole you get stuck and cannot sell? Your broker and the bridging provider together will make sure that you can switch onto a Buy-to-Let mortgage or similarly appropriate loan rather than stay on the bridge forever, facing conflict with the bridging provider and risking losing the house.

Chapter Twenty: How To Price A Refurb

If you are a new to property and new to flipping houses, then one of the key questions to which you need to know the answer to is:

"David, how do I work out the refurbishment costs when I am viewing a house?"

I hear this question very often, sometimes from friends out there in Property World on the Facebook property forums. Very often, I'll see an answer from someone who is trying to be helpful, providing the suggestion "Take a builder with you and get them to do an estimate". The problem with this is that you don't know if you will be offering on the house at this point. You are just doing a first viewing and you might be doing 20 or 30 such viewings before you find a property to make an offer on. It's just not a real world solution to ask a builder to accompany you through all of those viewings when **a)** there might be no work for them in that project, and **b)** they already have other work to do. They are simply not going to do it and so you have to develop the skill of working out the costs of a refurbishment yourself.

This is important – really, really important. The viability of your flip projects depends on you getting this right.

The skill, and this comes with experience, is to be able to work out how much needs to be spent on a property in order to bring it up to good lettable condition. Only when you have an idea of what is required and the cost of the work can you then work out what the house is worth. Only when you have worked out what the house is worth can you then calculate the offer and in turn, only then can you know that you are going to get a great margin when you flip the house.

The issue is that you may have never priced a refurbishment before. To help, I am going to give you an easy process to follow so that you can get this right. Even if you don't get this 100% accurate at the start don't worry as you'll still be able to put together some sensible numbers that will work for you. If you then use my Three-Scenario system to work out your margin, then even on a bad day, even if you make a mistake, you will still have left yourself with a margin of error that will ensure you won't wreck the deal.

The first thing you need is some kind of viewing spreadsheet. This is basically a list that you can apply on a room-by-room basis and which allows you to record exactly what the condition of the room is that you are viewing at the time. You can make one yourself on your laptop. Just make sure that you include every item you are likely to find with potential for needing attention or repair within the room that you are in. If you do this yourself, then this resource will be free.

You might also consider signing up for one of the multiple online resource centres and training providers that will provide you with the information and templates that you need. Many of these resources will give you access for a free 30-day trial and I suggest you take this up. During this period, I highly recommend that you undertake several viewings so that you familiarize yourself with what is required in many circumstances in any given room of the house whether it is a bedroom, a kitchen or a bathroom. At the end of the 30-day trial you have a choice to continue with the report provider on a paid subscription basis and if you are doing a lot of viewings then I would recommend this. This is something we do and we are delighted with the resource and flexibility of our online provider, obtained at a very reasonable cost. If you are right at the start of your Investing and Flipping journey then you might feel that after having looked at what is available then, at the very least, you are better prepared to put your own inspection spreadsheet together.

How do you use the online resource sufficiently to get the information you need during the 30-day free period? In other words, if you are just starting out, how do you know that you will do enough viewings in the first 30-days to extract the information you need? I suggest that you do what I did. In the early days, in order to practice compiling an inspection report I carried out an inspection on my own house, my brother's house, my mum's house, a friend's house... you are beginning to get the picture.

By the time you have completed half a dozen inspections you will be so much better prepared to do an inspection for real, out in the real world and you will start to feel so much more confident about the process.

A typical room in a property might look like this (I will start in the living room for this example). The carpet might be old and worn, normally in orange and brown with swirly patterns, an American shag-pile from the 1980's. There is an unpleasant wallpaper in place that may have looked really on trend and fashionable at the time it was put up (but probably didn't) and it needs to come off the walls today. There may be a rather grubby Artex ceiling from the 1980's – it used to be all the rage, especially with the semi-circle "comb" pattern. It was always a decorator's nightmare, even when it was new because to get a decent paint finish on it you had to follow the pattern of the comb lines, which took hours.

I tried it once in our new home in 1982, where the main bedroom had this patterned Artex in place. The lovely Mrs S decided that the ceiling had a white matt finish and she would like to have a white satin finish – the cutting edge in decorative choice at the time. I volunteered and gamely set about the task on a DIY basis. I moved the furniture about and covered it with crisp new polythene dust sheets bought specifically for the task from our local DIY superstore (which no longer exists today). I launched myself up a ladder with roller suitably loaded with paint and, well, it soon became apparent that a roller was not the appropriate tool for the job. The paint was splattering everywhere. I wasn't getting paint into the thinnest parts of the swirls. Instead I needed a paint brush and so ransacked the house looking for one. The only paintbrush I had in the house was a one-inch version and it was in a bowl under the kitchen sink, only a little bit stiff.

I had no idea what was on it, but I thought it would be fine once it had softened up a bit. Thirty minutes later I was getting nowhere. An hour and a half later and I had still covered only a tiny fraction of the ceiling, laboriously following all the comb shapes with my one-inch brush. After three hours I gave up, almost in tears now from the sheer boredom of the task. Looking at the ceiling I convinced myself that no one would ever know; a white ceiling is a white ceiling after all. However, as you all know, I was wrong. For the next three years I would lay in bed looking up at that white ceiling, half of it in a neat shiny, satin finish and half of it very neatly painted but in matt. We moved in 1985 and for all I know it still looks like that today.

Back to the living room of the house we are viewing. What do the windows look like? What are they made of? What are the window frames made of? If they are wooden and single panes of glass, then they will need replacing. If the windows need replacing, how much will that cost? The best way for you to find out is to call a couple of local, non-national window companies as they are more likely to help you on the phone. If it is a two-bed Victorian terraced house, then just ask "In round figures how much would it cost to replace the windows on a two-bed Victorian terrace?" There might be just six windows, a front door and a back door. They know the cost as they will have done this job dozens of times, and they will give you a "do not hold me to this" price.

Back to the viewing. Are there any stains or discolouration under the window bay or around the chimney breast? What about on other walls in the house? If there are, then there might be damp issues in the house and a report on the damp might be required. I always found it useful to carry a small, cheap damp-meter in my bag. These aren't the ones that the experts use but I find that they do work and they are helpful to have. You can get one online for £20-£30 and if used correctly, it will indicate if you need to investigate further. If you do need to get a professional in, then you can generally get a damp report done by a local contractor for free. Warning – local damp proof specialist companies make their living by finding damp and treating it. They may be a little more diligent than required in a real world situations and may suggest extensive damp treatment for your flip. You will need to take a view on their recommendations and whether you heed them. They will usually lead you to the worst of the damp and suggest that some treatment may be required.

You may then need to warn the vendor that you will need to make a further appointment for members of your team to come for a more detailed look. This shouldn't be a problem as long as you prepare the ground at the start and only get the minimum number of further visits in place. Try not to bring an army of tradesmen through the house preparing quotes at different times, instead try to coordinate the visits otherwise the vendor will get fed up.

Back to the viewing. What do the electric switches and visible wiring look like? In any event it is really important to ask the vendor to guide you to the meter cupboard so that you can see how ancient the meters and associated wiring are and how badly they may need updating. Does the property have a relatively new consumer unit? A rewire on a two-up, two-down, Victorian terrace where I work, will probably cost in the order of £2,500. Obviously it will be costlier for a larger house and you should speak to an electrician who is local to where you are. They might also suggest a ballpark figure to you on the phone.

If you want to get rid of the Artex, then the ceilings will need re-skimming. If you want to get rid of the old wallpaper then usually, in my experience, the paper will take a lot of the plaster off the walls with it. That plaster could be decades old and might be blown in several areas and this is one of the times when, in my view, trying to save money just doesn't work. Patching in old plaster with new plaster always means that the finish is compromised and is very labour intensive. You are better off to re-skim the whole room, which I always allow for in my estimates. Again, where I work this costs between £300 and £400 per room.

Re-decorating can also be estimated fairly simply. Depending what part of the country you are in, there will generally be a rate per room that can be used as an estimate to get the job done. Do not skimp by using cheap paint as if you use better quality paint then you will save on labour because it will require less coats to cover. Be sure not to let the decorator water down the paint unless it is done in line with the manufacturer's instructions. If they put too much water in, then you may as well have used cheap paint in the first place.

One of our decorators used to sing while on the job, to the tune of an old soup commercial from the 1970's. "You get more paint if you water it down, much more paint if you water it down". He doesn't work with us anymore.

In terms of flooring, I suggest that you find yourself a local flooring contractor. They will help you to pick the right specification, and in our two-up, two-down example I know that we can get the job done for around £800 to £1,500. The actual amount you spend will depend on the area, the tenant profile if you intend to keep the house, or the final price you are targeting for your flip. If you are looking for top money at the end, then you would need a higher specification carpet with a big, fat underlay.

If the boiler needs replacing it is very unlikely you will go for a top of the range model, and you will more likely consider middle-range or entry-level boilers. My views have changed on this and I always used to select middle-range boilers. The thing is, they break down anyway, so today I'm all about entry-level boilers. The cost of one, in my area, fully fitted without too much pipe work having to be updated is around £1,000.

Now you have done your inspection and you have a grasp of the works required. You have done your research and you have priced up the work. A very important tip at this stage is to always give yourself a margin of error and add in a contingency. I usually add 10% to the cost of the works that I have in my mind. At least this way, I know that I won't go far wrong and it's a pleasant surprise if I don't have to spend it!

You now have a grasp of the potential cost, so what do you do now?

The next step is that you need to work out the total cost of any works in terms of how they will affect your offer. We have talked about forming your offer in a previous chapter but generally speaking, if you consider paying around 60p in the £, based on your final refurbished value for the house then that should be pretty close to the correct number to offer.

One of the most important things about this process is that you must not rush it; take your time! I learned this the hard way and in the early days I let my business partner take control of pricing the refurbs. He is a lovely man but he can be a bit impatient, a bit hasty, and you never get anywhere if you are too hasty.

In the early days we had a couple of mishaps along the way. The first was a terraced house in Hanson Street, where he had priced-up the costs of refurbishment without really noticing that there was a bump in the middle of the living room carpet. It was quite a localised bump and you had to walk up one side and then down the other. It was about the size of a dead body hidden beneath the carpet but somehow it had escaped his attention.

The purchase completed and once all the furniture had been removed, the bump stood out more clearly and we had to investigate, with some trepidation as to what we might find we went in. It was a costly but great learning experience. Under the carpet was a chipboard floor. The bump was very obvious and whatever was causing it was beneath one particular sheet of chipboard. What could it be?

We removed the chipboard to reveal an original flag stone floor. You don't see many of these but I have to admit that I have seen a few. I always check for them now by jumping up and down and digging into a corner to see if I can find floorboards. With a flag stone floor there are no floorboards and the problem with them is that the slabs are like a sponge. The suck up water and the sheet of chipboard had warped because of the damp. Disappointingly, there was no dead body.

The previous owner had clearly laid the chipboard to try to stop the damp rising temporarily but it hadn't worked. There is only one way to fix such a problem, and you have to dig up the flag stones and take them away. Sometimes you can sell them to a reclamation yard for a few pounds – then in their place you lay a concrete floor throughout. After that, you lay a layer of asphalt on top of the concrete to stop the damp rising. It works but it has a cost and it probably added £1,000 to the refurb cost.

You see my point now; you never get anywhere if you are too hasty.

Chapter Twenty-One:
Refurbish, Don't Renovate

We have to be really careful in terms of how much work to undertake on a property. A refurbishment should be just that; what we don't want to do is to rebuild the property. Ideally the project we will be looking at would be one where we can go in, redecorate put a new flooring down and put the property right back onto the market again. Sometimes just a thorough clean-up and a really good scrub around the bathroom and kitchen areas will bring it up like new anyway. Those are the projects that are just golden if you can find them, and are a really cost-effective way to use your resources. Time is money, and the less time you can spend on a refurbishment means you can maximise your profit at the end.

The other thing which sounds obvious, but which is forgotten by so many friends going into flipping properties is that you should always plan your refurbishment and your cosmetic uplift to suit whoever it is going buy the property. Let's assume that you have managed to secure a three bed semi-detached house in a family area. Once you have completed your refurbishment, who is likely to be the customer for your property? Clearly you are going to be catering for families who want to live in that area in a family home. In those circumstances you should target your refurbishment so that it accommodates the needs of a family. Let's assume that there are going to be two adults and two or three young children living in that house. You have to target the refurbishment for them and their needs, not for yourself and yours. Do not get too creative with respect to your choices on refurbishment. For instance, families need a family bathroom, and if they have small children they will need to put them in the bath. Walk-in showers and wet rooms are fantastic if you are dealing with young professionals whether living on their own or as part of a couple. They will really like high quality walk-in wet room showers and won't need a bath. However, if your target market is going to be families, then you must include a family bathroom in your refurbishment.

Similarly, in a family home you are going to need some form of entrance lobby. You need a porch but you have to make sure it is protected from the weather. It will ideally be an area that is inside the house but that does not encroach on the main living area. It will be a form of lobby area where the kids can leave their Wellington boots and their coats can be hung up and wet things can be left to dry, without being taken into the main living area of the house where they can spoil carpets and decorations and furniture.

At the other end of the spectrum, if you are working in the middle of the city and you have managed to secure a loft apartment that has lots of stairs, it's more likely to be suitable for young professionals to live in and you don't have to worry about space for kids' wellies. What you would need then is your bijou walk-in wet room with a fantastic shower. You will need plenty of concealed storage, very clean minimalist lines and to make sure the colours that you use are appropriate for modern day living. You might even go for hardwood flooring rather than carpet. No one is going be disturbed by children racing around on hard floors and making a huge clatter. But to the contrary it would be really cool and appropriate for young professionals living together in their first home; a city-centre loft apartment.

Keep your eye on the budget at all times and remember your margin. You should work out your plan in advance and stick to it throughout the refurb. Do not become emotionally involved in the refurbishment and do not put things into it that you like, that are appropriate to your taste that you would choose if you were going to live there, if your target market would need to change things when they move in. The reaction you are looking for, whether it's a family home or a loft apartment for young professionals is that when they walk in through the door, the first thing they say is "wow".

Keep your eye on the budget at all times. The target has to be for you to add £3 of value for every £1 that you spend. You will not get there every time but it is a very good target to have.

Chapter Twenty-Two: Setting Up Your First Investment Property And Your First Tenant

We've looked at the flips, but what about the houses to keep and rent out which are key to building our own property empire? To make sure they work properly and that the rent from the tenant will service any mortgage that we put in place, we have to make sure that the tenant that we get in, is a worthwhile tenant. If you pick the wrong tenant, someone who knows the game and who might try and game you, then you lay yourself open to losing control of your property because the tenant won't pay the rent, won't look after the house and won't leave at the end of their contract. If that happens, you are going have to sort it out.

All of that stuff *can* be sorted out and when you are an experienced landlord you will get to know how to do it. However, there are steps you can take in the early days that ensure you will get a good tenant who pays the rent and looks after your property.

Don't forget that part of our early research included having detailed conversations with local Letting Agents. You should go back to them once you've completed your refurb and ask them to look after your property. You may be tempted to manage the property yourself as many landlords do. I personally don't, and the reason I don't is that I really don't want to be a letting agent. What I want to do is get out there, do some more deals and earn big money. The landlords who look after their own properties clearly take pride in doing so and I am sure do a great job, but I don't think it's an efficient use of time. You can get a really good letting agent to manage your property for a fee, in my experience, of between 8% and 12% of the monthly rent. In an area where the monthly rent is around £500 a month then you are paying £40 to £60 per month for the letting agent's services. Personally I think this is exceptional value for money.

The other thing you have to make sure not to do, is to try and knock down the fees of the letting agent, as this will be very counter-productive. If you have a good letting agent, you have to look after them as they will make you money. Don't worry about knocking 1% or 2% off of their monthly fees because the sum you are going to save is tiny compared with any voids, any significant repairs and any rent arrears that you could suffer in a poorly managed property.

These are the sort of jobs that a typical letting agent will do to set up a tenancy. First they will draw up particulars of the property on behalf of the landlord and then market the property, both in their shop or office but also on one of the online rental portals. They will conduct any viewings required by prospective tenants. They will filter out any unsuitable applicants whether their unsuitability might be financial or otherwise. I don't think you want to be meeting tenants at all sorts of odd hours to do these viewings, do you? I am sure that on a good proportion of these appointments for viewings the prospective tenant doesn't show and it is just a waste of your time. Remember that the Letting Agent does all of this within the charge included in his or her fee.

The letting agent will then take up any references required prior to the tenancy and will follow them up by speaking to former landlords and employers and any guarantors that you require to be put in place. In my experience as a landlord, you should definitely make sure that a property-owning guarantor is in place for the tenancy that you set up. Having this in place gives you a failsafe if things are to go wrong at any stage, and I always ask for a property-owning guarantor to be put in place on any of the tenancies for my properties. I cannot tell you hand-on-heart that I have never been knocked by a tenant and there are indeed occasions when the rent has not been paid and I have not been able to recover it from a tenant. However, I can tell you hand-on-heart that I have never been knocked by a guarantor. On the rare occasions I have had to write to a guarantor seeking funds from them in line with their promise, the money has always been paid.

Once all the background checks have been put in place, the letting agent will make sure that an up-to-date, compliant Assured Shorthold Tenancy agreement is signed and put in place. On moving day, the letting agent will attend and check the tenant into the property making sure that the tenant is familiar with all the appliances and everything that needs to be done to make sure the house works efficiently. For a small additional fee, the letting agent can also arrange for an inventory to be done on the property, and I very strongly recommend that you have one of these put in place. At the end of the tenancy, if there is any disagreement about the condition of the property then the inventory will show a clear written record with photographic evidence of the condition of the property when the tenant first moved in.

The letting agent will also take a deposit from the tenant and register it with an appropriate deposit scheme. At the end of the tenancy this deposit will need to be returned to the tenant if the property is still in good condition, subject of course to reasonable wear and tear. If there is any dispute between the tenant and yourself over the return of the deposit monies, then in effect you will have no chance of winning the argument and a deposit scheme will return the monies to the tenant unless you have an inventory and photographic evidence in place.

If you are determined to do all this work yourself, and want to manage the property yourself, then of course you can do it. If you are going to take that route, then I would very much recommend that you join a national landlord's association. Indeed, the options are for you to join the RLA (the Residential Landlords Association), or the NLA (the National Landlords Association). There is an annual subscription to be a member of either of these groups, and at the time of writing it is around £75 per year. It is a very valuable resource and you get access to all of their pro-forma documents, everything you need to run a tenancy. You also get access to their legal helpline which will be invaluable to you if you suddenly find that you have a problem tenant. Even if you are not managing your properties yourself I would recommend joining one of these associations. It is a great resource of information, up-to-date news and a sympathetic ear when you need one as a landlord.

Now your tenant is in and the tenancy is up and running, make sure that you receive your monthly rent statements. When you do receive them, make sure you read them. I know that sounds obvious but I have found over a period of time that some landlords don't check that they've had their rent in on time. More than once I've had phone calls from landlords in some distress who tell me that they haven't received any rent for six months. How can this happen? What is everybody doing? Why has nobody taken any action? You need to run your investment property like a business and I am all over rent arrears as soon as they start. The longer you leave it, the larger that sum is that becomes outstanding and then the less chance the tenant has of being able to catch up.

In my own world this is how I manage rent arrears in my portfolio. If one months' rent is missed, we need to know why. Most tenants are very good, and if there is a problem for one month it can be for several different reasons. I would always listen and be patient with them at this point and give them the opportunity of bringing the account up-to-date. However, when a second payment is missed we have to be a little firmer. I ask the agent to issue what is known as a Section 8 notice. This can be issued when the tenant is two months in arrears in rent payments. Please note this doesn't mean that you have to wait for eight weeks before you issue the notice. Because rent is paid in advance missed rent payment could come as little as 30-days after the first missed rent payment. It is at that point that you issue the notice. It is at that point that usually the tenant brings their affairs up-to-date.

Sometimes the tenant still cannot bring their affairs up-to-date. If they communicate with you, at least you have the opportunity to try to help if you wish to. However, sometimes tenants just go very quiet and leave you with no idea as to what's going on in their world. If I don't hear within 14 days of issuing a Section 8 notice, then we have the right to go to court and asked for a court hearing, the result of which might be a court order for repossession of the property. There is a cost to this and any application to court at this point may well cost a few hundred pounds. If you are a member of one of the national landlord associations, then you can use their paperwork and get free legal advice on how to proceed. It will cost you nothing and they will give you up-to-date advice which is first class. On the other hand, if you are working with the letting agent then they may also have their own system for dealing with this and you just have to prompt them to start the Section 8 process.

Some letting agents will only serve Section 21 notices. A Section 21 notice is a completely different tool designed to do a different job and can be issued in any circumstances and at any time, and ultimately it guarantees the landlord getting possession of the property. However, it does not give any opportunity for the landlord to pursue the rent arrears which is why in a rent arrears situation, I would use a Section 8.

One thing I always do myself is go to court following a Section 8 notice if we are seeking possession of the property. It doesn't happen very often but when it does happen I like to go along and most usually the tenant doesn't attend. I don't want you to get the wrong impression about what going to court is about in these circumstances. It is not how it looks on the TV and you don't sit in a public court room with people watching and the judge sitting up high looking down on you. That would be very intimidating. What happens instead is that you finish up in an office with somebody who is acting up as a judge on the day, usually a solicitor or a local barrister. You tell them the story and ask for possession. The situation is that if you go to court seeking possession under a Section 8 notice, and the tenant is in arrears for at least two months' rent payments, the court is obliged to give you possession. They have no discretion in the matter at all.

We've come quite a long way in the course of this book. We know that investing in property over time can make us wealthy. We know that we need to flip properties to help us fund our investments. We've looked at where we should buy and we've looked at what we should buy. We've looked at the type of properties we want to invest in and we've considered the type of properties that we need to flip. We understand what a deal is and we've started putting our power team together comprising estate agents, an accountant, a mortgage broker, a solicitor, builders and everything we need to make out new property business work.

We know that we are going to start out by flipping a couple of deals to generate the cash to make our first investment. We've also looked at buying through the estate agent and buying in an auction. Those are the places where most people start.

We've looked at selling at an auction. We've looked at funding the deal whether it's from the Bank of Mum and Dad, joint venture finance, or working with a bridging lender.

Now maybe it's time to move on. Maybe it's time for me to introduce to you some of the more advanced ninja strategies that will turbocharge your cash-flow. This is my story and this is what happened to me. This is how I used flips to build my portfolio and then I moved into one of the most compelling cash-flow strategies in the industry today.

I'm going tell you a little bit about my property sourcing and packaging business.

PART 2 – MY STORY

Chapter Twenty-Three: Show Me The Money (Part 1)

In property I am now regarded mainly as a Deal Packager and I'm not really buying property any more. I have chosen to source great deals and place them with investors for a fee as the main part of my property business. That is how I make my living today and that is how I pay my bills.

This section of the book will show you how to earn big fees fast in the world of property and in doing so you will need no money, nor will you take any risk. You can earn big fees from selling houses that you don't own, to investors who are building their property empire.

But this book called "Get Into Property" and not "Deal Packaging – How to do it" so why am I taking the story in this direction? It is because in the real world, in my story, the transition from flipping houses into packaging deals just seems so natural that one flowed from the other. The skills are the same and you can use the skills we have discussed in Part 1 of this book and use them to grow a large cash-flowing Deal Packaging business.

Why Get Into Packaging Deals?

What you need to remember at all times, is that what I was in property for was to generate money. I needed cash in my life and maybe you can relate to that? Now of course, I wanted to invest for myself and build a portfolio of property that would grow over time, but it soon became apparent that I needed cash-flow in my life and needed money, both to fund the investment purchases and to support my life. My premise in this section of the book, is that flipping houses and flipping deals are very closely related. They are intrinsically linked to each other, in fact the mind-set for both is virtually identical. For any newcomer starting out in property, if you're investing in your own portfolio, if you are going to start flipping houses to raise cash to support your investment purchases then it is a tiny step before you can start sourcing properties that other people will buy in order to generate cash for you from the fees that will flow.

If the purpose of a flip is to raise cash, then you don't have to buy the flip yourself and sell it on into the market to earn cash. What if your profit, taken in "flipping the deal" on to an investor and letting them buy, refurbish, and sell the property was the same amount of money or even more than can be earned in going through the process yourself? In my property business, in every deal, the most important thing is to find the way in which I can earn the most money for the least amount of effort.

That is why I got into Deal Packaging.

This is why you should get into deal packaging as well. You can earn as much money from a deal by not doing the deal, but by passing the deal to somebody else who will pay you a fee, as you can by doing the deal yourself. The thing about deal packaging is that you get paid on day one, as soon as the property has been purchased by the investor. Furthermore, you are only using the same skills that you have developed in sourcing your investment properties and your flips.

It is the most efficient way to earn money with the minimum amount of resources and effort in the property industry today or at any time during my journey through property. If I can't place the deal with an investor, then of course I can do the flip myself. However, I like an easy life and I've already got the investor, I've already got the deal, so why don't I just get paid for passing it on? Then I can use that money to fund my own investment purchases.

That is what happened in my life. That is what happened in my property journey, and that can easily happen to you as well. I want you to understand that the power of packaging deals to other investors and the cash-flow that runs from that will support your life financially whatever other strategies you regard as being your principal strategies in property.

There is a very firm view in the world of property regarding what a Deal Packager is and what it is that they do. I am going to challenge that view in this book. I am going to explain exactly what it is that a Deal Packager does and the hope and intention of writing this section of the book is to change your mind-set so that you may understand better how you might be able to package deals and earn handsome fees by doing so.

I want to help you.

It is in that change of understanding that the magic happens, and you can move from struggling to set out on your property journey to a place where you are earning money in property. Whatever your main strategy is, I want to help you get to a place where you are confidently placing two or three deals a month with investors and you will be earning tens of thousands of pounds in the process. Most importantly you can do this alongside your main strategy. You can earn money selling houses that you don't want to buy.

What This Is Not

I need to make this very clear. I believe that the vast majority of people think that Deal Packaging is, in fact Deal Sourcing. My contention is that Deal Packaging and Deal Sourcing are very different. There appear to be hundreds of Deal Sourcers out there in property land and the common view is that most of them do a poor job.

That is probably because they *are* doing a poor job.

Is this familiar to you? Maybe you are on a Deal Sourcer's list? Maybe you get regular emails from someone who styles themselves as a Deal Packager but is in fact just a Deal Sourcer? Maybe you open their emails and read the headlines of one of their deals?

They will always tell you that they have sourced a house which is "20% BMV". Now, I struggle with the concept of BMV, a property that is Below Market Value. Suffice to say at this point that I don't believe in the concept of Below Market Value and I never use that phrase in my business.

I don't even really understand what people mean when they use the term BMV. I mean, I understand in general terms what they are trying to convey but I find the concept of BMV an elusive one. I know that others don't believe me when I say that, but it's true. Below market value is a very specific term, that implies that the market value for a property in a particular street is set, and that you can ascertain what it is very easily. Then you can very easily decide whether your property has been sourced BMV or not. In my experience that is not how it works.

Let's assume that I find a property that is available, and I need to find out if the price it is offered at is below market value. When I have a look on the property portals, maybe on Rightmove, Zoopla or wherever else, I can see the transactions that have been carried out in the street over several years and I can see the prices that have been paid. What does this tell me? In a typical street what it will tell me is that the houses are all very similar but that very different prices have been paid. Now there may well be good reasons why different prices have been paid. In a typical street in north-east Manchester you can find houses that have been sold for £40,000 or for £80,000 and anything in between, all in a similar time period. Why have these houses achieved different values, and what does this tell you, if anything about the value of the other houses in the street?

There are many reasons why different houses sold at different prices at different times. It might be their condition. Some were likely very smart and some could have been very rundown. Without physically going and looking around them, there is no way that you can tell which is which. Maybe the vendors at the time of the sales had different pressures upon them. Maybe there was urgency in the sale and maybe there wasn't. Maybe some had a lot of equity in the property and maybe some didn't. Maybe those that did have equity were in a position to take a lower offer because they wanted to get on with their lives somewhere else. The point that I am making is that just looking at these transactions cannot guide you to the open market value of the properties. As such, you cannot decide whether the property you are looking at is below market value or not.

It gets even more complicated when we get mortgaged properties involved because at some point the mortgage company is going to get a valuer to come in and look at the house. In my experience what the valuer does is that he or she will look at the most recent transactions of very similar properties in the street or close surrounding area. It may well be that the most recent sale was a very low figure relative to the other sales figures in the street. Nobody but the parties involved will know why this house was sold for a low figure and maybe there was something in the vendor's life at the time that prompted them to sell cheaply. This very low figure will likely affect the valuer's view of property prices in the street as a whole. The low sale price might even be viewed as setting the new open market price for the street. That reduces the value of every other house in the street, and resets that number at which the term below market value can be applied.

On any given day, what is below market value? Who knows? It's not quantifiable and so the term has no place in my business.

Everyone loves a discount and I get that, but my issue is in how to quantify whether we are getting a discount and what exactly the discount is.

The "deals" on the emails that really tick me off are the ones that offer a property at 20% BMV and suggest that you can buy a £100,000 house for £80,000. However, they then go on to say that there is a refurb required and when you have a look at the refurb it is likely to cost in the region of £20,000. New electrics, new plumbing and boiler, new windows and doors and a new damp proof course are all required, so in effect they are asking you to pay £100,000 for a house which is worth £100,000. And they expect a fee for that?

When you do your research you can see that these properties are not actually "20% BMV". In fact, they are nowhere near 20% BMV because the research put into them has been shoddy or selective. You have had a look yourself and you might decide using your criteria that the property is offering a discount to the market value of around 7%. Then, because you have to factor in the sourcer's fee and the 7% discount to the market, it all but disappears. Depending on the state of the market, in my experience it is not hard to secure a discount to the market of around 7% just working with an estate agent. If you are talking to an agent who is offering a house at £100,000 then they will expect to accept an offer. If you offer £93,000 then you will have secured your 7% discount. Job done.

If they are not working with estate agents face-to-face then many Deal Sourcers appear to spend their time online, scraping the property portals and looking for deals that are being advertised online with an estate agent. What they are doing is just sending out to a list of potential investors, details of houses that are for sale in an estate agents office. They may have no connection nor control over that property at all. They haven't even viewed the property. They send out someone else's property with a price they haven't agreed on it at that moment in time, and then ask for a fee for sourcing it.

What they have done is to break the very first rule of Deal Packaging and that rule is:

To serve your investor you have to find a property deal that will add value to an investor's life and then pass it on to them for a fee.

What This Is

My concept is slightly different and very clear; I am going to put forward the proposition that Deal Packaging is actually flipping houses. That is what the strategy is at its core.

If you want to be a Deal Packager then at the core of what you do must be the understanding that the service that we offer has, at its very heart, the concept of a flip.

The accepted view in the industry of a flip, is a property transaction where someone buys it, adds value to it and then sells it back into the market at a profit. This type of transaction, start to finish as we have discussed earlier has some risk attached to it. Did you buy at the right price? Will the upgrade go over time or over budget? Will the market have changed while the project is in progress?

This will not matter if you are in an upward cycle in the market and the rising market will always get you out of trouble. If the market is faltering, then at the end of the project you could have done all that work and be looking at a loss for all your time trouble and effort. It happens.

Investors have made handsome profits over the years following the flip strategy. I know that you will too when you follow it. However, there is some risk in setting up a flip, especially if you are new to the industry and have never done one before. You have to get your numbers right and make sure you are working with people that you can trust, not least the builders.

What if I told you that there might be a better way? What if I told you that you can make good money by flipping a house where you don't have to buy it, don't have to finance it, don't have to raise Joint Venture funds, or bridging finance, or use your own funds? Where you don't have the responsibility of finding and dealing with builders, and you aren't affected by the vagaries of the market place. None of these things will affect your profit in the deal. You will get paid in full, and at the start of the project. You can take your money and run. All you have to do is find it and introduce it to an investor; you have NO RISK in the project.

The other thing you need to remember is that all the skills you need to source your properties and flip your properties are exactly the same skills that you need to source and sell your deals. You are already doing 99% of what needs to be done to start a deal packaging business and that is why I fell into it so easily. It was a tiny step for me to take the properties that we were being offered and to get third-party investors to buy those deals instead of me, and to pay me a fee for sourcing those deals in the process. That is why I wholly recommend to you that you should consider sourcing and selling deals to 3rd parties for cash-flow.

Many don't want to do this right at the start, and I understand that. You may feel this way too. At the start you will be busy enough searching for properties that you want to flip, and that you want to add to your investment portfolio. I'm telling you though, and I've been there that before very long the reality will dawn upon you that you can earn cash by not buying houses, and that is a very attractive proposition.

That is Deal Packaging.

Deal Packaging is in effect the ultimate primary strategy for every deal you will come across. You will be securing a deal and moving it on to an investor. The investor will have their life enriched as a result, and in return they will pay you for your efforts in finding and securing a deal for them. Crucially though, that is where your responsibilities will end. The investor will fund the deal, they will fight through the legal process and they will work with the builder to ensure that the potential of the project is realised. Of course you may wish to assist the investor in their endeavours going forward, but in doing so your fee will be increased accordingly.

If we aren't going to talk about BMV in our outsourcing business, then you may be wondering what exactly it is that we are going to offer our investors. In my experience the concept of BMV is something that new sourcers talk about with new investors. Any seasoned investor who knows what they are doing is far more interested in the Return On their Capital Employed (ROCE). As such, we need to talk about the concept of ROCE in our conversations with investors.

What is ROCE? If you aren't familiar with the concept it is very simple so allow me to explain. Let's assume that the investor has some money in the bank or a building society. The amount of interest that they are getting on their money is tiny and they have been in that position for something over nine years now. At the same time the official inflation rate in the UK is significantly higher than any interest you can get in a bank or building society account, which is a worry for all investors. Investors are smart and they know that they are struggling for those reasons.

By introducing them to the concept of investing in property, you are immediately giving them the opportunity to stop the losses they're effectively accruing on their savings, because their money will be invested in a bricks and mortar asset that will go up in value over time. At the same time, you are using the income that you will receive from the tenants to pay any bills, including mortgage payments that need to be paid to run that property. To work out what the ROCE is on a property is quite straight forward.

All you do is take the net profit on an annual basis from running the property and you divide it by the amount of money that the investor has put into the property. Your net rent, after all costs, may be around £250 per month. That will add up to £3,000 net profit over a calendar year. In this example, let's assume that the house in question has cost £100,000, but the investor will have bought it using a mortgage. The total capital at the time of writing employed in the purchase of the house might be the deposit which is likely to be in the region of £25,000. In order to calculate the ROCE on this purchase all we have to do is to divide £3,000 by £25,000 and express it as a percentage. If you do the calculation, you can see quite quickly that the net return on the investor's money has now gone up from virtually zero in the bank or the building society to a very solid 12%.

This is achieved without implementing any of the advanced techniques that you will learn in the course of your property journey which may enhance the income for a house like this even more. For the time being let's just talk about letting houses to families on an Assured Shorthold Tenancy, and then we can work backwards from there.

The presentation of the deal to the investor is very straightforward and you just need two bits of paper. Let's talk through how you would go about presenting the deal outlined above. On both pieces of paper, you should start by having the figure £25,000 written at the top. On the left-hand piece of paper you should write beneath it the amount of interest that is earned from the bank or building society. At the time of writing this book that interest could be in the region of 1.5%, which would generate total interest over a year of £375. On the right-hand piece of paper, you should point out the figures that could be achieved if that £25,000 was invested in a bricks and mortar asset, a house. As we've seen above, the return on that capital in the house purchase would be around 12% and would generate income before tax of around £3,000 for the year.

This is the power of property and this is what we want in our own lives. This is why we are attracted to investing in property in the first place and this is why we carry out our flips so we can generate money, and so that we can invest in property later on. We have been attracted to property because we want these sort of returns in our own lives, and bear in mind we aren't even taking into account here any capital growth that we may achieve over time just by holding that property in our investment portfolio. The sum of all these benefits is what we can offer to our investors, since they want these sorts of returns as well.

What you need to understand is that once you are up and running, and once you are being offered properties by estate agents and your contacts, then what you will want to do is buy your own houses for flipping, buy your own houses to keep as investments, and to sell the ones that you don't want to third-party investors, getting paid a fee as a result.

This stuff isn't difficult. This stuff is easy. Let's get started.

Chapter Twenty-Four: Moving Forward

At this point, let me return to the story of my experiences in property.

We were on our way and had reached the stage where we were buying houses almost on a weekly basis, but life was different then. Finance was very different then and it appeared that anyone could qualify for Buy-to-Let mortgage. There were self-certificated mortgages available for the self-employed and business owners where basically if you could just confirm that you could pay, you were in. It felt like if you could mist up a mirror by breathing on it, then you could get a mortgage.

We bought and bought, and sometimes it felt like we were buying chocolate bars rather than houses. However, we only had a limited amount of cash for deposits and we were quickly ploughing through that. With a rapidly rising market we relied heavily on the Buy, Refurbish, Refinance, model that we are taught at Progressive Property. That works for sure, but it is inevitably true that you generally don't get all of your money out, and a small proportion of your deposit funds remain stuck in the deal. After 15 or 20 deals we were running out of cash.

The thing is we had built a fantastic network of suppliers for properties and various individuals were sending us deals on a regular basis. We had also hooked up with the most trustworthy builder in the world to do any remedial works required. We had even recruited our own Girl-Friday who was everywhere on a daily basis, doing our viewings, liaising with the builders and generally being our eyes and ears on the ground.

Helen (as was her name) had been living in one of the houses that we had purchased and we met her through that. She was between jobs, and as a gift to the vendor she had volunteered to stay in the property and improve it cosmetically so that it might achieve a better price in the market. She did a really good job. When we got talking she sold us on the prospect of employing her to work in our business to do the things that we could not do. Don't forget, we were living in Brighton and this new property venture was in Manchester. While Manchester is a great town, neither of us wanted to live there. The prospect of having someone who knew her stuff, or at least enough to move things forward and who could provide us with updates on a daily basis, was a very attractive prospect. For that reason we quickly put her on the payroll. It was very informal at first, with the two of us agreeing to split the cost of having Helen on the team, but the value of having her involved became significant.

It ended of course, as all these things do. There were several reasons but in part it was because in her personal life she had this thing about plumbers. She really liked plumbers and in return, plumbers really liked her too. The thing is when we recruited a new plumber then her interest moved on to the new recruit and she ultimately left a string of unhappy plumbers behind her. We had no idea that all this was going on, but we did think it strange that it had become increasingly difficult to find a decent plumber to come out and service our new property empire. It was only after the event that we found the truth and understood why most of the plumbers in North East Manchester were no longer taking our calls. They don't teach you this stuff on the property training courses!

We had built a modest, but in our heads effective little machine for sourcing deals, with a couple of great mortgage brokers for getting the finance over the line, solicitors that we could work with and builders who could do anything we needed doing. We even had our own Girl Friday on the ground who could be our eyes and ears and could look after our stuff, but there was a still a problem. As I alluded to before, we were running out of deposit money. All our original funds were now "left in" various purchases and deals.

We had put a deposit into every deal at that time, because that was how we thought you had to do it. We had no knowledge of any "creative" strategies, because we were self-taught; "we didn't know what we didn't know".

For instance, we had no idea that some of our property investor friends were using "Day one" re-mortgage strategies for 100% of the purchase price so that, in essence they purchased a house without a deposit. They didn't need a deposit. It wasn't just about the deposits either. The situation was that if you purchased a house at, say, 25% below the full market value from a distressed vendor then on the same day as you completed the purchase, you could, through the magic of the legal process, draw down funds based on the full value of the property. It's unthinkable in today's financial climate but back then it was all the rage. The bottom line was that you could buy a house with no money and based on the re-mortgage value you might even come away from the purchase with extra cash in your pocket too. This extra cash could add up to several thousand pounds and it wasn't taxable as it was in effect, debt on the property. Hopefully you can understand that it was a quite a popular ruse.

As with all ruses, it is not the principle that was the problem but the abuse of the principle that prompted disaster and its demise. Some property friends regarded the extra drawdown on the "Day one" re-mortgage as income and not debt. They spent the money, they bought cars with it and they sustained inflated lifestyles with it. A few that I know got so deeply into this strategy that for them it became about buying a house a month, any house, so long as the numbers worked out for the extra drawdown. These houses were bought cheaply and needed upgrading to become good lettable houses but the money wasn't spent on that; it was just spent. If they needed more money, then all they had to do was to buy another house.

There were friends of mine that had a target of buying two houses a month just to maintain their spending. Of course, this process was brought to an end by the crash of 2008 but it left those friends high and dry. They couldn't buy and take money out of the purchases any longer and at the same time they couldn't rent out their houses because they'd never brought them up to lettable condition. The conditions of the properties were so bad that you couldn't put decent families into them. I knew one property investor at the time who owned 77 houses and of those, 17 were unlet and unlettable. He had no money to bring them up to standard so that he could get some rent coming in from them. That model for a portfolio would never work and alas, financial disaster was inevitable.

Fortunately, we didn't know any of this while it was going on. Nobody told us about it, and ultimately it appears that not knowing this strategy served us really well. The reason is that when the crash came in 2008 it really knocked property prices in the North of England in particular. Prices dropped in some areas by as much as 40%. Unlike those investors who had followed the "Day one" re-mortgage model and had done so irresponsibly, we had put the required deposit into every house we bought and we had invested to ensure that they were all in good lettable condition and we were fully let. We had regular income and when the interest rates came down to an historic 0.5% during 2009, we were set fair and secure from the icy storms of the financial recession or depression or whatever it was.

Back in 2005 the point was that we couldn't buy any more since we'd run out of money, but we were still being offered all of these great, cash-flowing properties in the North West of England. Here was the dilemma; should we say to our estate agent buddies "No, I'm sorry but we've run out of money. We will be interested, but we won't be in a position to buy again, well...for about a year". We thought that-that wouldn't go well and considered that if we went down that road then we would just drop off of any "special" list that we were on and would soon be forgotten. Instead, we hatched a cunning plan to keep ourselves moving forward. We would start talking about the opportunities that we were being offered, with friends, family and everyone we knew back home in Brighton.

We would start to offer them the opportunity to leverage our contacts, our power team, our boots on the ground and our contractors (well, unless they needed a plumber). In fact, we would leverage everything that we had put together in the North West over the previous year or so. When we were offered a property, we would build a group of potential purchasers back at home and would allow them to buy the house in return for paying us a fee. We were starting a Deal Packaging business. We didn't even know it was called a Deal Packaging business and we certainly didn't know how to do it properly at the time but we were on our way.

Chapter Twenty-Five: Doing Some Deals

We started out pretty quickly really, but what you have to realize reading this book today is that the atmosphere and the financial climate and the world in general was very different in 2005. The world seemed to be obsessed with property, everyone wanted to buy a house and all sorts of people approached us to get onto our investor list.

The proposition for them was that they could use our contacts and power team to build a property portfolio for themselves. The attraction for us was that we could continue to use our new infrastructure and contact base. The new investors would use their money to buy and refurbish the properties, plus they would pay us a fee for our services. We had no ongoing interest in the property but instead our interest was in the fee that we would receive as the legal process was completed and the investor took possession of their new property. We sent them an invoice and they paid.

So how did we attract the new investors?

Well we mainly just started talking about what we were doing, and the people came. We spoke to family and friends, we spoke to accountants and solicitors, we spoke about it on the golf course and we spoke about it while having coffee. We didn't realise it at the time but what we were actually doing was "content marketing".

Content marketing is one of the most powerful tools that you have to attract investors to your property business, and it still works as well today as it did back then. You can see other people doing it on a daily basis using social media, and in particular on Facebook. Back in 2005 we didn't use Facebook and so it had to be face-to-face, but today you can leverage social media and reach tens of thousands of people on a daily basis with your message. It doesn't have to be a sophisticated message either. All you have to do is to share with other people what you are doing, take some pictures of houses that you are flipping, share some numbers and give your readers the opportunity to dissect the numbers in the deal. You can do a walk-around video of a completed project, and if you do create and share content on a consistent basis then people will come. Back in 2005 we had to do it by word-of-mouth.

We started talking about our journey socially and it was a little bit like Facebook content marketing as discussed above, aside from the fact that we weren't aware of Facebook as a marketing tool at the time. I'm not even sure if Facebook was a marketing tool at the time, but in any event I certainly didn't have a profile. We would talk about the area that the property was in, the infrastructure and the regeneration plans. Then we would talk about the arithmetic behind the deal; the cost of entry, the purchase price, the likely rental return, the gross yields (at that time still comfortably in double digits) and the return on capital invested over time. We focused mainly on cash-flow as the reward for investment but there was certainly the prospect of capital growth over time as a further incentive to purchase.

We got a bite or two quite early-on, and the sales went through. We over-cooked the fees in the early days perhaps, but fees of £4,000 from a single let in a reasonable area were commonly paid. And then a strange thing happened; our early-adopter investors became our best marketing tool as they started speaking to others about their purchase. The spoke in glowing terms and started to introduce us to their friends which was something I hadn't expected. Now, I am sure that they were genuinely happy with the returns that they achieved but for the first time I came across a phenomenon called "pride of ownership". How it works is if somebody makes a purchase, especially a major purchase, then obviously they want to be recognised as having made a smart decision in making that purchase. If they have made a smart decision then it is likely a decision that they want everyone else to know about because it makes them look smart. People like being known for being smart.

Brighton is not very a big town. There are maybe 150,000 or so people who live there, but it is really a small town. Everyone knows everyone or they know someone who knows everyone and so inevitably, word started to spread. The coffee bars on Church Road in Hove, some of which doubled up as our HQ, were alive with chatter. You mustn't forget that all of this was against a background of a desire in British society to buy property, especially at a time when finance was easy to secure and plentiful and anyone could obtain it. Every day the newspapers were talking about property prices going up in the region of £10,000 per week. We were starting to build a reputation to the extent that some people who, a year earlier, had listened to us patiently but decided that what we were offering just another "hair brained" scheme which wasn't for them, were now starting to come forward and ask "Now then… these old houses you are buying up in Oldham or whatever, what's the story?"

Momentum was building, people were talking and we now found that we were selling houses for a fee. Within just a few months the focus in our business had moved from sourcing and investing for ourselves, to sourcing for others for a fee, and this was really profitable. We had no financial commitment to any of these deals. We were not raising deposits, getting mortgages, seeking joint venture partners, making applications or doing everything else that was required to put the finance in place to buy property. All we were doing was leveraging our teams in and around Manchester that we had built over the previous 12 months or so, and the investor was buying the properties. At the end of the process the investor paid us a fee. As we moved forwards, we found that we could do two or three of these deals per month. The fees at that time were around £3,000 to £5,000 per deal. This was cash-flow we hadn't anticipated coming in from our property business and you can understand how it got our attention.

Chapter Twenty-Six: Scaling Up

We now had people who wanted to buy, but the issue was that we needed stock. We learned very early on that there is always an issue in balancing stock and demand in any Deal Packaging business. Either we found we had stock and no customers, or we had customers waiting and no stock to offer them. As I will cover later, by far the most comfortable position to be in for any Deal Packager is to have lots of potential customers and no stock, which is where we found ourselves. We had loads of demand, and investors waiting but we couldn't find the houses quick enough. We had to get busy.

We carpet bombed the estate agents in and around North West Manchester; "What have you got? I've got cash buyers waiting. Hurry up and find something for me". The properties were just not coming fast enough, added to which prices were being pushed up on a near-daily basis (or so it seemed).

Programmes on TV which were about making money in property, began to dominate the screens and I could sit at home and watch Sarah Beeny, Kirsty and Phil and everyone else who wanted to launch a property TV show, explaining to the masses how to do it.

The effect on the market was extraordinary. Prices were going up fast. In and around North West Manchester, houses that had taken nearly 2,000 years to reach a value of £40,000 now were going up by £10,000 a month. Investors would agree to buy a property, and while they were going through the legal process on the way to ownership, the property would have risen in value. Hindsight is a wonderful thing, but at the time we couldn't see any problem with this. We believed it was an upward correction to the market, i.e. that the market in this area had been suppressed for so long that all that was going on was a long overdue return to normality.

We had educated and reasoned conversations with estate agents and property colleagues within which we argued that this correction was permanent and logical and that any house in this area should be worth £100,000 or more. Clearly it was obvious to all.

So, onward we went but now it was time for the hard-yards. There was no stock at a time when everyone wanted to buy houses. Everyone was in the game, and speculators in the property market were now beetling up the M6 motorway and invading the estate agents' offices. We didn't have enough stock to fulfil demand.

We thought that we had better find another way of sourcing houses and so I appointed myself as the Chief Officer in charge of Auction Acquisitions. Maybe we could get enough stock there? I quickly found that this wasn't going to work either. Traditionally auctions were the places where property professionals plied their trade and they weren't for amateurs. If you wanted to find a deal you could find one there, but you needed to take care because these were shark infested waters. It was also the place where property professionals got rid of their mistakes.

The issue now was that all the TV watching property heroes now turned up at the auctions and started bidding. Inspired by Sarah, or Kirsty, or Phil, the butcher, the baker, the candlestick-maker, they all turned up at the auctions and started bidding. No longer was this space the preserve of the hardened property professional, quietly plying his or her trade and nicking stuff for a song. Prices were now retail and the general public were bidding way too much for very ordinary properties. Auction houses were no longer wholesale, trade environments, they were definitely retail with prices sometimes going higher than on the High Street. They were also places full of danger and disaster to the untrained property investor.

Going Wholesale

On the face of it we were facing difficulties. We had people queuing up to buy, but what were they going to buy? We couldn't get enough deals from estate agents and auctions weren't going to work either. We had demand for houses, but then again so did everyone else and the market was being driven up by the media and by easy access to finance. What to do?

When I say that we couldn't find enough deals from estate agents, there was one agent who did try. This is a guy who worked for an independent estate agent in Oldham and who was at this time, selling ten houses per week, which is significant. He was eminently qualified to be an estate agent. His previous roles involved working in the Slumberland bed factory assembling beds. He'd then moved on to work in a local abattoir. His time in the abattoir wasn't wasted and he rose at a meteoric rate through the ranks of the staff who worked there. Ultimately he was appointed to the coveted position of "pig head boner"; those of you with experience in that industry will know that this was a role that ideally prepared him for a career in property. He went on to join the local estate agent where he became a master in the art of selling houses, and was soon the leading salesman in the office.

That is when we met him. He tried to keep up with our demand but the instructions weren't coming through fast enough. We followed him all over town viewing various properties, during which time we some very ugly stuff. He was doing well because at the time you could sell anything. Sales of ten houses per week brought him a lot of commission and many bonuses in the office including a BMW M3 in a bright blue colour. You could always spot when and where he was doing viewings, not least because he insisted in parking the BMW in the middle of the road wherever he parked so as not to scuff his high-spec, low profile alloy wheels on the curb.

Eventually the conversation had to be had.

"It's no good lads, you won't get there quick enough waiting for me. Why don't you go and see this bloke, he might be able to help you" he said in his broad Lancashire accent.

This was the breakthrough moment. He introduced us to several professional property traders that he had worked with over a period of time, and set in motion a chain of events that meant we had access to trade sellers of property in and around Manchester. This was the moment when our business took off.

We met all sorts of characters over the next several months, all of whom were firmly entrenched in the wholesale part of the property business in and around Manchester. Some of them were a bit dubious and we inevitably had to sort the good from the bad, but there is no doubt that the good ones helped us to build our business and to grow.

One of the strangest property wholesalers that we met was M.

M had smart offices and we went to visit him for the very first time, feeling excited and nervous at the same time. We enjoyed a good old chat but on that occasion he didn't have anything in stock that was suitable for us. However, he told us to keep in touch because new stuff was coming in all the time and he was sure that he could help us going forward. The other person that we met (and clearly this individual was key to M's business) was M's personal assistant Wilson. Wilson was a very thin man, also in his 50s. He looked a bit crumpled and down-at-heel, and whenever I saw him he was always wearing a long, black, heavy overcoat. It didn't seem to be connected to the weather or to the time of year. He always wore the same long, black, heavy overcoat.

It became clear over several visits to see M for coffee that we weren't going to get any business done here. Events on our final visit to M's offices came as a bit of a surprise but we took the view that perhaps we were better off spending our time elsewhere in our search for wholesale property leads. It was quite a chilly winter's morning as we pulled into the car park behind M's offices. We were quite surprised by what we saw. Wilson complete with his long, black, heavy overcoat was tied to the railings that ran along the back of the car park while M was hosing him down with a garden hose. To say we were rather taken aback is an understatement. What could possibly be going on?

M greeted us with a big smile invited us into the office, leaving Wilson out in the car park tied to the railings in the freezing cold. He sat us down at the desk.

"I'm afraid I can't offer you a tea or coffee" he said. "That is Wilson's job and he's going to be tied up for an hour or so. I will let him in in a little while and he can organise a brew for us"

We had to ask **"What is going on?"**

It transpired that M had sent Wilson out to collect some rent. Wilson had called in on a couple of reluctant tenants and had collected the rent payments in cash. Unfortunately, on his way back to the office it was necessary for him to pass a local bookmakers shop. The inevitable happened since it appears that Wilson could not pass a bookmaker's shop without going in. The only money he had on him was nearly £1,000 of M's rent that he had collected from the recalcitrant tenants. Wilson duly placed some bets on a horse which came in last.

By now M had relented a little and had decided to allow Wilson back into the building. I suspect that it was more because he wanted a cup of tea rather than out of concern for Wilson's well-being. Wilson arrived in the office looking a little soggy, and while he was in the kitchen area I sought him out to make sure he was okay. He was still wearing his long, dark overcoat, still very wet and steaming gently.

"Are you okay?"

"Oh don't worry about me. I am fine" he said. "It's all my fault. I've broken the unwritten law. I deserved my punishment. Do you both take sugar?"

To be fair we didn't have many appointments like that.

One of the most valuable sources of wholesale property that we found was as a result of a direct introduction from our estate agent friend in Oldham to a new contact, Joe. Joe was a member of a very Orthodox Jewish community in Manchester. It is a community that is quite large and active but which keeps itself to itself.

Many of the members of that community are active in property. Just spending a day on patch with them is very instructive in how to work with estate agents and other sourcers who might have really good deals. Being active is the key, and these guys were busy. They were on Rightmove and the other property portals every single day looking for new listings, and when they found them they followed them up. They never let one go even if on the face of it the property didn't really fit their criteria, or look like a deal. It was a masterclass in being persistent and in chasing down a deal. If you do what they do, you will find properties to buy for your own portfolio, to flip, or to sell for a fee to an investor. The deals are out there; it is just a numbers game which you must make sure you play.

They are tireless in their journey, and what many would consider normal working hours, seemed irrelevant to them. I remember one evening I was sitting in our flat in Ashton-under-Lyne, the base for our property business as we moved forwards. At about a quarter to midnight the telephone rang and it was Joe who had a property deal to talk about. We went through the process and discussed the deal in detail before arranging to meet the following day to do the viewing.

I felt that I had to raise the issue of the lateness of the hour with Joe at the end of our conversation, and I made it clear:

"I am always happy to speak Joe but you do know that it is 11.45pm? I'm not in bed or anything, I am only watching TV but it is a bit late."

"It is not a problem for me David. I work all the time... I work 24/6".

There is a lesson for us all there!

I duly attended the viewing of the house the next day, and met with the owner of the house who had also come along to meet us. We entered a conversation and it soon became clear that this gentleman not only had a very significant portfolio of properties, but that he had made the decision to get out and sell everything. The owner just wanted rid of them and he wanted rid of them fast. He had big plans and wanted to launch a new venture outside of property. He needed a lot of money to launch it.

He had dozens of little terraced properties, exactly the sort of thing that our investors were looking for and the locations for most were okay. In honesty, the condition of these houses was terrible but the price was right and we were also offered the opportunity of picking and choosing which houses we wanted and placing the houses incrementally. We didn't have to take them all in one go which was key for us.

It was this introduction that changed our fortunes and set us on our way. With the modest team that we already had in place, Helen and Tony (the most honest and trustworthy builder in the world) we set about picking the best of the bunch and then selling them to our investor database and bringing them up to good lettable standard. The Deal Packaging fees that we generated from this portfolio set us up. The sale of these houses brought in sustained fees over a period of time and gave us the time we needed to find other sources of houses. We decided this was the way to go.

Of course, there were new challenges that we found along the way too, the main one of which was keeping everyone happy. As we scaled up we had to work with more people. We needed more builders (certainly more plumbers) but one major issue with working with more builders is that you become anxious to maintain the flow of work to give them since you know they need to work. You know that they too have responsibilities and staff to pay every Friday – for some reason builders appear to be paid weekly on Fridays. If you don't have a project for them to start when they need to start, then you might lose them off site. If you lose them off site, then you have no idea when you might get them back again.

We found that we needed them when we needed them and we knew that projects were in the pipeline once the legal people had done their stuff. The pressure therefore, to keep the builders busy was real. I have to say it did prove a bit overwhelming for my business partner on more than one occasion and we had to deal with the fall out and sort it all out.

We had been buying house incrementally from the gentleman, our trade supplier mentioned above. We had picked off the best ones and we were now definitely dealing with the second tier of houses in terms of them being in quite poor condition. We had put in an offer on a house, which had not quite been accepted but we felt it was a foregone conclusion. At the same time one of our main contractors was coming to the end of a project and needed more work or we would lose him. Inexplicably my business partner decided that as the acceptance of our offer would be a foregone conclusion, then there would be very little issue in sending in the building team at this stage to commence that rip out of the house, and it was a massive rip out. The house was in a dreadful state and everything had to go. Out it all came and it finished up in several skips. The skips were whisked away. What my partner didn't know was that the owner had a plan to sell this house to a different purchaser at a higher price. We knew nothing about this alternate buyer.

The owner of the house arranged a viewing with his third party and hadn't expected to see what he saw. The house was completely ripped out; carpets, rubbish but also the kitchen and bathroom had all been ripped out and taken to the tip. The owner was livid. One of his complaints was that this had destroyed the possibility of him selling to the third party at a higher price because the prospect wanted to buy with a mortgage. With no kitchen or bathroom, the house was not mortgageable.

The owner wanted everything reinstated, the broken oven, the horrible smelly carpets, everything. That wasn't going to happen because it had all gone to the tip. To be honest just stripping the house out meant that it was in a better state than when we had found it. There were several angry phone calls, solicitors were involved and threats were made of going to the police because of potential acts of criminal damage. It all went away in the end and we went through with the purchase for one of our investors.

Learn this lesson well; when you get up and running it is vitally important that you *do not* strip out someone else's house. They might be understandably upset about it. Whatever the pressure, *do not* send your contractor in unless your investor has bought the house or you have negotiated a key holder agreement with the owner and confirmed it through solicitors. This was a real lesson learned for us.

Chapter Twenty-Seven: Building A Business

In spite of these early hiccups, our business picked up apace. We agreed to buy, refurbish and sell over 20 of this owner's properties over the next 12 months. It was the break we needed to get our business up on its feet and we had fees coming in. We still had our contacts within all the estate agents, and we had more and more people who wanted to buy our deals. The business just took on a momentum of its own. When we were back in Brighton all sorts of people were approaching us and they wanted to buy houses in the North West. They were looking for cash-flow. They were looking for low cost of entry into the market.

We even held a Property Investor day at hotel in Brighton. We hired the really nice room for a day and we managed to get 38 people into the room to hear what we had to say. We gave them lunch, and all of the prawn sandwiches went first.

Amongst the 38 people who attended, there were delegates who were never going to buy anything from us. For instance, my Mum came just see what we were up to and she ate some prawn sandwiches as well. When we had a good hard look round the room we decided that there might be 24 people there who might be interested in buying some of our deals and who would have the funds to move forward.

To be fair, we put on quite a good show for them. We brought several property professionals down from Manchester and they were able to share what they did with those in the room. We had a mortgage broker, a letting agent, a small developer and a wonderful young woman who specialised in housing the homeless. We gave a full day's content to the delegates who came along. This isn't something that you could do every week and in my view we exhausted all the contacts we had locally to fill the room with the 38 people that came along. Just to give you some idea of the numbers, I estimate that the Investor Day produced deal packaging fees for us in the region of £80,000 and it is a gift that keeps on giving. We are still working with investors today who want to buy our deals, but these people weren't in that room, however their friends were. We are now working with their friends, and also the friends of their friends. Recommendation and referral is a very important part of your business if you are selling deals or if you are doing flips and you are trying to raise finance to get your flips over the line.

One of the delegates, a good friend of mine came to me during the morning and said "I'm really sorry David but I'm going to have to leave early. I need to leave at lunchtime. You see Brighton and Hove Albion are playing at home this afternoon and I am a season ticket holder. I wouldn't want to miss the match".

Well what could I say? I wished him a very pleasant afternoon. I don't have a season ticket at a football club myself, but what I'm led to believe is that when you have a season ticket you sit in the same seat for every match. My pal sat himself down in his regular seat preparing to watch the game and the gentleman who always sits in the next seat next to him also arrived to sit and watch the game. A light conversation was struck up between them.

"What have you been up to?" the neighbour asked my friend.

"Well I've been to a seminar this morning by a couple of guys I know who are selling really interesting property deals in the North West of England. The cash-flow seems to be really good."

"Wow! I need to talk to them." His neighbour said. *"That's just the sort of thing I have been looking for."*

That is how it works; word-of-mouth is your best advertisement. Of course we did end-up working with the season-ticket holder at the football ground and we have also worked with one of his friends. Once you are up and running and you have flipped a few properties and shown a profit, why don't you hold your own property investor day? You too can earn £80,000 from a day in a hotel that might cost you under £1,000 to put on.

Chapter Twenty-Eight: Compliance

You've got to do the right thing in the right way, so I have to start this chapter with the serious stuff.

I have shared with you how it is that I came to Deal Packaging by doing flips, and I am strongly recommending that you should do that too. Once you understand how financially rewarding it can be then you will be all in, I am sure of that. The immediate issue is that once you cross that line from flipper to Deal Packager, the law puts a guiding hand on your shoulder and steers you towards compliance. You have to be compliant.

I love the fun bits of this property business. The fun bits for me are meeting estate agents, doing viewings, making offers, meeting with investors, speaking to architects, meeting with structural engineers, lining up builders, agreeing a deal, tracking it through, adding up the fees in the pipeline (probably no more than five or six times a day) and checking the cash in bank. The main Key Performance Indicators (KPI's) in my business are cash in the bank and cash in the pipeline. If either of those appears to be dropping and the reason for that is non-specific, i.e. I have not spent it on something, then I know that activity is required. Activity is the key to success.

More specifically, focused activity is the key to success and it is the same in any business. If you are making sausages, then you have to be feeding sausage meat into the sausage machine in order to get sausages out at the other end. If there is a gap in the process, then your sausages will suffer and you will produce poorly formed sausages. Do not get wind in your sausage machine; you don't want to get wind in your sausages as you won't be able to sell them and make money. At the same time, I am informed that you don't want to get sausages in your wind-machine, but I think that's a topic for a different book.

There is absolutely no doubt now that the activities of Deal Packagers are regulated in the same way that estate agents' activities are regulated and this is under the Estate Agents Act of 1979 as amended.

This is a very serious matter as we all have to be straight and legal. To be absolutely clear, you will only find me preaching the word that we have to be compliant with the legislation and I am going to share with you the minimum criteria that you need to fulfil in order to be compliant. There is much more than I am going to share with you here because this book is about making money. The steps I am outlining here are the bare minimum that you need to do to be compliant. This information will keep you straight and legal and you can work without worrying that there will be a heavy knock on the door at some point and that "they" will drag you away. That will not happen, but I say now loud and clear that you must have these matters in place in order to lawfully carrying on a Deal Packaging business.

There is indeed a cost to putting these provisions in place and in total I estimate that you can do the whole thing for under £1,500. If you are standing there, on Day One of your property career then I would say that you do not need to do this stuff yet. To begin with you aren't going to be packaging deals, remember? You are going to be flipping and buying for your own portfolio. It is only a bit later as you grow and follow the money that this stuff needs to be done, and by that time you will have the cash in the bank from several flipped properties.

What Do You Need?

First of all, you need Professional Indemnity insurance. The reason why of course, is that it is sensible and good practice for any business that conducts itself in the activities of guiding and advising investors who might be considering a property purchase to ensure that the advice it gives is accurate. Not all deals go to plan, and in fact if you are working in property then the deal probably won't go to plan. Something unexpected and unforeseen will happen. Something that you might have expected and foreseen but thought that it could not possibly happen again, will happen.

Part of my presentation, my script when I meet with new potential investors for the first time, addresses this. I always accompany every presentation of a deal that I make with these words.

"Now these are the timescales that we are working to and this is the budget that we expect. However, you should know from the outset that whatever is agreed between us, we will go over time and we will go over budget. We have never finished a project on time and to budget. As long as you are happy with that, then this is going to be great"

There are investors who think in that moment that I am not being serious, but I am. There are also investors who thank me for being so upfront and candid, and from their previous experience they usually understand the issues involved and how the overruns and over spends can occur. In a modest, light refurbishment such as a cosmetic upgrade with new flooring, then time and budget is not an issue. That is quite easy to organise and finish on time, but over the years I have become involved in more testing projects. Much of the work we do is taking Victorian terraced, two-up, two-down houses and transforming them into five or six-bed, all-en-suite HMO's. I can tell you that when you are taking apart a house that was built, say, 130 years ago then all sorts of unexpected issues are going to appear. Major unanticipated works can be required.

For instance, we undertook a project very similar to the above, converting a two-up, two-down terraced house into a five-bed, all-en-suite HMO in a quiet street in Oldham. We had no idea, even after a structural engineer's report that after we had stripped the back wall of the house back to brick that all sorts of stability issues would be revealed. It was complicated further because we needed to add a kitchen extension and join it to the house. It was more critical because the plans allowed us to place a dormer-window in the roof at the rear of the property under permitted development which would place even more loading and stress on the rear wall. Building Control were consulted and their view was very firm. In order to fix the problem then we had to rebuild the rear wall of the house and in order for it to be properly supporting the extra weight then we had to strengthen the foundations beneath it first. We had no idea how testing this would be. Building Control insisted that the foundations could only be placed on top of firm ground, and in this area of Oldham, firm ground meant we had to find clay.

Down and down we went, well I say we but in fact it was the contractor who took this on. And I say it was the contractor but actually it was John, a newly arrived labourer from Romania who was charged with the task. He went looking for clay, and down and down he went. He couldn't find clay. He found all sorts of other things, lost Tudor galleons and the remains of Roman centurions but alas, no clay. He was now 9 feet below the level of the ground and still digging. Nothing. Every day he would come to work and was lowered into the hole. He didn't come out again until going-home time.

Still no clay.

We were actually considering hiring a pile driver to accelerate the process, with all of this going on in the back yard of a terraced house in Oldham. Finally, John hit the hard ground and we could start building upwards again. Today you would never know what had gone on. The project is finished, licenced, occupied and in great condition, ready to face the next 130 years. The slight issue of course was the added cost. The whole episode had increased the overall budget by £17,000; ouch. It was really nobody's fault but the lesson learned for me here was that maybe I needed to be creating a different type of accommodation.

Anyway, back to the topic at hand; so, should you obtain Professional Indemnity insurance? I have looked and I cannot find anywhere a legal requirement that says that Deal Packagers need it. Good practice aside, I don't believe there is a legal requirement for Professional Indemnity insurance, however, there is a legal requirement for Deal Packagers to join a legal redress scheme. There are a couple of them operating at the time of writing but the one that I joined is provided by the Property Ombudsman. In order to join the Property Ombudsman redress scheme, a requirement is that you have to have Professional Indemnity insurance.

The Property Ombudsman (TPO) is also very specific about the amount of cover that you need; a minimum of £100,000 of cover and a maximum excess on the policy of £1,000.

This can be a little inconvenient because in my experience the industry offers "off the shelf" type policies with blanket cover. Policies that I have seen generally offer cover of £250,000 or more with an excess of £1,500, which can be a problem. If you do as I did and just send the application to the TPO with a Professional Indemnity policy with an excess of £1,500 instead of £1,000, then they will return your application to you. The insurance provider however, generally offers standard terms and will not change the excess for you so that you can register. You will be relieved to know that there is a tool to fix this. You need to ask your insurance broker to get the insurance provider to add the policy endorsement "L1391 – The Property Ombudsman endorsement – excess £1,000" to the policy document. There is in my experience, no extra charge for arranging this and this will be sufficient to support your application for membership. Sorted.

The point of the TPO is that a client can go to them with a complaint about your service. However, there are strict rules about when a complainant can go to the TPO to complain about you, for instance they must have exhausted your internal complaints procedure first before they can go to the TPO. This obviously requires you to have your own complaints procedure in place. I have seen online, out there in property-land, property friends fretting and gnashing their teeth as they try to put a suitable client complaints procedure in place, but you don't need to fret about this. The TPO, with great consideration for your predicament provides a template for you on their website. Once you have joined you can go onto their website and download a pro-forma template complaints procedure. You can then just personalise it for your particular business and... job done. Well done TPO.

The next thing you need is to register with the Information Commissioner's Office (ICO) since you will be acting as a data controller and you will be processing personal data. Even if you exchange business cards with someone at a property network meeting you will have control of some elements of their data and will need to register with the ICO. The cost of registration is very small. At the time of writing, for someone starting out then it is £40pa or £35pa if you pay by direct debit. The online form is quite short and your membership is granted instantly if you apply online. Why would anybody not register when the process is so simple and inexpensive?

The fourth thing that you need to do is to register with HMRC to comply with their Money Laundering regulations and this is a requirement. The online process is a bit complex and it can take ages for HMRC to respond, but once your application is submitted then you are on your way.

Together with the form comes a 61-page guidance document which contains all the information you need to make sure you are compliant. It isn't a very exciting read but it explains how it is a legal requirement that all Estate Agency businesses, including Deal Packagers, must have a written policy statement together with controls and procedures to show how the business will manage the risks of money laundering and terrorist financing identified in the risk assessments. For every client and for every transaction a risk assessment has to be carried out. You also have to ensure that your customer due diligence includes identification checks for sellers, buyers and beneficial owners before entering into a transaction with them. You also have to check on the funds that a new investor might have in place, and verify the source of those funds.

I have covered the basics here, and if you do these checks and keep records on what you have done, then you will be fine.

It is very easy for friends new to the industry to get completely distracted by the issues of compliance. Of course it is important and the regulations are there to protect everyone involved, but it is a massive subject. Do what you are supposed to do and put the basics in place and read all the guidance. Then we can get on with the main thing which, dear reader, is for you to start earning money from your new property sourcing business.

That is where we are going now.

Chapter Twenty-Nine: Show Me The Money (Part 2)

Once you get started with your property business you will be really surprised at how quickly things can move forward. This was our experience and this is what happened to us. In this chapter I am going to share with you a few sample deals that we did in our early days to show you how quickly things can start to happen.

The thing about Deal Packaging is that, as with every other strategy it can become very detailed and complex when you've been through the starter strategies and you want to build a Deal Packaging business. I am not going to talk about the advanced strategies in this book, since the premise for it is to get you started quickly and earning money whether you are doing flips, buying your own investment properties or sourcing deals for other investors.

The best way that I can illustrate how you can make a quick start and then move forward is just to walk you through the journey that we took so that you can see how this stuff works.

I would strongly suggest that your focus at the beginning should be upon sourcing houses. You should be sourcing the very same type of houses that you are looking to do your flips with, as those that you want to put into your investment portfolio. It makes it such great leveraged use of time if you can source properties that you want yourself, when you are also looking for houses that you can sell those to investors for a fee. With this in mind we are going to start with the process of finding a house and then we can move through the process and see how your business should grow.

Finder's Fee

One of the very first properties that we sourced was a house in Balfour Street, Oldham. We went into our favourite estate agent's office, (you remember the guy with the BMW M3?) and he said to us:

"Would you like to have a look at this? It has just fallen through for the second time."

Absolutely we needed to look at that. Whenever an estate agent says to you the house has fallen through for the second time, you need to go and have a look. Why did it fall through? Is there a problem? Can you ease the vendor's pain by placing it with an investor?

On this occasion there were no issues with the property at all. It was immaculate and a young couple had lived there for some ten years. The house was presented like a little show home. Within the previous 12-months they had been spending money on this house and had put in a completely new shower room. The issue was that Mrs Vendor had fallen pregnant and was expecting their first child. They didn't want to have the baby in this house and although they had been very happy there for around ten years, they didn't think it was big enough to start a family in. They put the house on the market and sold it pretty quickly, or so they had thought.

The difficulty was that they chose to market the house at the very same time when mortgage lenders were really tightening up the criteria for first time buyers looking to buy a property. This had meant that prospective buyers had been unable to raise a mortgage because although they loved the house, they were first time buyers and could not proceed.

When the young couple first put the house on the market, Mrs Vendor was only slightly pregnant. However, six months had now gone by and she was now quite a bit more-pregnant. She was getting very anxious because they had placed a reservation fee on a new build property, a three-bed executive home, which was being built on the outskirts of town. They thought that they wouldn't be able to sell the house, that they would lose the opportunity of buying the dream home and that the reservation fee would be lost. Could we help?

The house was being offered at £65,000 and there was plenty of evidence in the street that this was the true value of the house in its immaculate condition. Remember though that everyone loves a discount and this deal really wasn't about the house it was about the people. They were expecting a baby and Mrs Vendor was now really stressed. They didn't want to lose their new dream home and they certainly didn't want to lose their deposit.

We made one phone call to one of our cash investors with whom we had worked previously. We explained the situation and over the phone the investor made a cash offer of £54,000. The young owners of the house accepted the offer and thereafter the sale moved forward very quickly because our solicitors understood the urgency, and the young couple were being represented by a solicitor who was a family member so he also understood the urgency. The sale went through and the young couple didn't lose the reservation fee of the new executive home. They had the baby in the new house.

From the investor's point of view, she got a really good deal. At this present time, she is organising a Buy-to-Let mortgage for that house. The house should value up at £68,000 which means that she will be able to pull £54,400 out of the property.

Of course, the investor had to pay our sourcing fee which in this case was £3,000. This type of fee for this type of deal is what's known as a Finder's Fee. What that means is that all you have done is sourced a great cash-flowing property at a discount to the market, and you can see how easy this was for us to do. It merely involved a visit to an estate agent's office and a phone call to an investor. For providing that service you are entitled to charge a fee and at the time we charged £3,000 for that type of deal. We would now charge £5,000 for that deal because that is the market price for sourcing a deal of this type and we believe in the properties we source. You can see that you only need to do a couple of those per month and most people could easily cash-flow their life like that. Go and source some Finder's Fee deals and earn yourself £10,000 per month.

Meanwhile the investor has acquired a great cash-flowing property and the house has been rented almost since the day that she completed on the purchase. As you can also see from the numbers she only used a tiny amount of her capital to push this deal over the line.

"But wait, David" I hear you say, "what about that poor young couple? They have dropped £11,000 by selling that house for £54,000. How can you sleep at night? How can you look at yourself in the mirror?"

To an extent I can see why you might think that.

When the transaction was done I received an email from the young couple. What they said in the email was "Thank you David. Thank you for all of your help." As a result of what we had done the young couple had been able to make their move to the new house, have their baby in the new house, everyone was well and very happy and they have been able to move on with their lives. They were grateful to us for the service that we provided.

What a great way to do business!

Pre-Packaged Deal

The next type of deal that we have sourced for investors is what's known as a Pre-Packaged Deal.

In my view, there is a sweet spot in Deal Packaging that includes Finder's Fee Deals and Pre-Packaged Deals. Those are the main strategies you need to focus on, and by focusing on them and just them you will earn the most money fastest.

Let's talk about the Pre-packaged Deal. We dropped in on one of our favourite estate agents one day and he said to me:

"David would you like to have a look at this? It's just fallen through for the second time."

As you know by now, the answer to that question is always **"Yes. Let's go and have a look"**.

We went to have a look, and you will remember that the first property discussed above was immaculate? Well this house was *not* immaculate. This had been a family home for over 50 years but everyone had grown up and left. Mrs Vendor had passed on a few years earlier and Mr Vendor was living in the house on his own. The house needed a complete update, but that wasn't the reason it wouldn't sell.

If you have a look at the picture above, you can see that there is scaffolding at the front of the house. The problem with the property was that the front skin of the front wall was moving away from the rest of the house. It was nothing urgent and not a cause for panic, it was just slowly and elegantly moving away from the rest of the house. In truth there was no immediate concern that there was an imminent danger of collapse but it's the sort of thing that mortgage companies don't like, and so two sales had fallen through because it wasn't possible for prospective buyers to get a mortgage on the house.

The house was in a very popular street. It was a really strong residential area, working people lived there and most of the houses were occupied by families. It was a really good street to invest in and the prices reflected that. At the time, the open market value for properties in that street in good condition was between £90,000 and £95,000. However, this house wasn't in good condition and so I asked the vendor what he wanted. He told me that he understood the problem, that he knew he had to find a cash buyer but that he needed to move. He couldn't manage in the house on his own anymore, and he needed to move on. He knew where he was going to go, it was all organised. In order to make the move he needed £50,000, and he went on to tell me that the previous week he had-had someone like me come and visit him in the house. The previous trader, knowing that the vendors needed £50,000 had made an offer of £48,500. The vendor was incensed and threw the trader out the house.

Now sometimes I can be a bit slow, but I'm not that slow. I thought about what the vendor had said, and I made a proposal to him.

"Thank you for showing me around the house, I would like to make you an offer also. The thing is I am not going to offer you £50,000 either. I want to offer you £51,500, because I want you to have your move and I want you to have a bit of extra money that you can spend on whatever you want to spend it on. Do we have a deal?"

We shook hands and the deal was done.

I called one of my cash investors and she purchased the house for £51,500. Now, the thing about this deal, was that it went a little bit wrong. The original plan, inspired by the investor was to buy the house, do all the work, bring it up to a really nice specification and then flip it back into the market for a profit. We would split the profit with the investor.

Why was this a Pre-Packaged deal? This was because we used our contacts and power team to do the works. The investor couldn't do this on her own as she lived 300 miles away, and so we brought our builders in to do the work. That adds value to our service.

The structure of the deal was very simple and the investor would produce all the money. We would get all the work done using our contact, while the investor would pay for everything. Then, when the house was re-sold we would split the profits between the investor on one side and us on the other side on a 50-50 basis.

Everything went swimmingly well. The structural work that was required at the front of the house was done over the course of a weekend and the front wall that you can see in the picture above was taken down to the level of the ground floor window and was then rebuilt and was checked and signed off by a structural engineer. We had his report in writing since we didn't want any more problems for anyone who wanted to raise a mortgage on this property going forward.

However, when the works were almost complete I made a mistake. As the carpets were going down I invited the investor to come and have a look at the property. We had done a really good job and I wanted her to see where her money had been spent. The difficulty was that when she saw the house she fell in love with it wanted to keep it. Now obviously, not for one minute was I concerned about my share of the 50-50 split of the profits in the resale and how I was going to get paid now that the house wasn't going to be resold. It was as if the investor was reading my mind.

"Don't you worry about your share of the profits." She said. "What I'll do, is I will pay you a fee of £10,000 which approximately is the amount of profit you would have made from this deal."

That is a Pre-Packaged Deal fee and as you can see it is higher than a straightforward Finder's Fee. This is justified because you've done more work in the course of the deal. You have leveraged your contacts and your team to get the job done and you deserve to get paid commensurately for that.

Those are the basics of the Finder's Fee and the Pre-Packaged Deal fee. If you just use those two strategies, you will make money from your new property business and more importantly, you won't be doing any more work than you will need to do to find your own flips, and to take those projects to the finish line.

The great thing is that you can scale these models up, and once you understand the service you have to provide and that people will pay you for that service you can move forward really quickly.

Let me give you an example of a Finder's Fee deal which carried with it a much larger fee.

We were doing our usual trawl of the estate agents offices in Ashton-Under-Lyne and one of them also happened to deal with commercial properties. The property in the picture opposite had just been put on the market by the freeholder.

It was an office building which was let to Tameside Metropolitan Borough Council and they were using it as an overflow from their main offices for various purposes at the time. The council were paying a high rent, around £75,000 per annum. There were nine years left to run on the lease.

One of our investors based in Brighton was looking for a commercial building to buy, and their criteria was that the tenant had to be a really strong covenant (the council matched that criteria) and that the lease gave the obligation to maintain the building to the tenant. Again that was exactly the situation with this building. The other box that we had to tick was that the investor needed to achieve a double digit gross yield on their investment. Ultimately our investor bought the building, paying in the region of £700,000 for their purchase. The gross yield on this building came in at between 10% and 11% so the client was happy since all their criteria were met. They agreed to pay us 2% of the purchase price as our deal packaging fee, which meant that we were paid £14,000 just for finding the opportunity.

This stuff is real and you can do it too. The problem with this last example is that it whetted our appetites to do bigger deals and to generate larger fees. This prompts us to ask, where do you go to find the bigger deals on a regular basis?

Searching For Bigger Fees

Put simply, you just have to ask! When I say you just have to ask, what I mean is you have to go on asking everyone that you meet. Someone will have the connection and will know the person you've got to speak to. They may not even know that they know the connection and the person you have to speak to, but if you just keep asking and pushing you will make that contact eventually. And so it was that we met Tarquin Ramsbotham. That isn't his real name incidentally, but it does encapsulate the magic of his name.

Tarquin was a Northern lad in his mid 30's, born and bred in Bolton. His parents were working class, he didn't come from a moneyed background and the story is that his dad decided to call his son Tarquin so that the boy would become a strong fighter at school.

We met Tarquin when we went to view a property in Ashton-under-Lyne. He was possibly the owner, but as I learned later in my relationship with him there was always a web of intrigue around every deal that he did. There is no doubt that the family had accumulated great wealth. They had a large import and export business and in the 1980s and 1990s Tarquin's dad had gone round most of North West England buying up abandoned and dilapidated old mills for £1, funded by the profits from the import and export business. It didn't matter how long they had been abandoned nor how dilapidated they were, nor did it matter if they were knee deep in pigeon droppings (which some of them were), Tarquin's dad would buy them if he could get them for £1. Some 20 years had elapsed and suddenly everyone in property wanted to be a developer. They targeted abandoned mills in the North West of England, and suddenly the Ramsbotham family were potentially wealthy beyond their wildest dreams, having bought these crumbling old wrecks for £1.

Tarquin's dad was really smart. The other thing he had done over the years was to buy up odd bits of land all over the North West of England, again funded by the profits from the import and export business. He hadn't done anything with them but had instead just put the deeds away and kept them.

This is called "land banking". The principle is that you buy up bits of land, usually at a time when the economy will not support developing that land, and then later on when the economy turns you build on the land and earn lots of money. That is what the Ramsbothams started to do, and it was about this time that we met Tarquin.

The property in Ashton-under-Lyne that we went to view the very first time we met him was a complete non-starter. It had a cafe on the ground floor which was very smart and very busy, and there were rooms above with separate access from the street. The rooms were full; in fact they were very full. There were a lot of people living in that building and even though we were relatively new on our property journey we could tell that all was not as it should have been in that residential space, with respect to regulations and so-on. We declined the opportunity to get involved in this particular project.

However, it was clear from our very first meeting that there was a mutual liking and respect between Tarquin and ourselves. There was a lot of laughter and it certainly got him interested enough in what we were doing to see if we could grow the relationship further. As a result, he invited us over to his offices in Bolton and sure enough the following week we headed over to see where this would lead.

Where it led to was a rapid growth in our Deal Packaging business. Tarquin was building out blocks of flats on the land banked bits of land that his Dad had bought over the years. He was extremely intelligent, very knowledgeable and as far as property was concerned, in my view, a bit of a genius. We learnt a huge amount about property, deal structures, JV structures, planning law and how to work with the planners, all from watching Tarquin operate. However, he didn't suffer fools gladly and was impatient and grumpy most of the time. He particularly enjoyed baiting my business partner who has many fine qualities including a tendency to wear his heart on his sleeve. DG doesn't have a poker face.

I remember well there was one particular afternoon when we had gone to visit Tarquin at a building that he had bought off Chorley Old Road in Bolton. It was a magnificent building, clearly having been built at the turn of the 20th century when Bolton was at its most affluent. It was a huge, magnificent structure in substantial grounds. Tarquin wasn't sure what he was going to do with it at this point, but for the time being he had made it into his HQ and had moved all his offices up to this building.

On this particular afternoon he seemed to take excessive delight in teasing my partner DG, to the extent that at one point during the conversation DG stood up and announced that he'd had enough, that this was the last straw and that he wasn't going to be treated like that. He stormed off in a huff, opened the first door and left the room slamming the door behind him. I was left on my own in the office with Tarquin and I wasn't sure what to do. Should I dutifully follow DG from the room or should I stay where I was and continue the conversation with Tarquin, knowing that that would lead to a stressful conversation with DG about where my loyalties lay, later in the day?

Fortunately, Tarquin took the initiative. He very calmly looked me in the eye and said:

"He'll be back in a minute".

How did he know? Sure enough, within 30 seconds (which seemed like hours while I was sitting there) the door handle started to turn and the door opened. The issue was that there were two doors in that room immediately adjacent to each other, and you must remember that this was our first visit to the building so we were unfamiliar with the layout. One door led to the landing and to the staircase out of the building. The other door, the one that DG had opened and stormed out of, led to a cupboard. I tried not to laugh but that just made it worse. What made it impossible not to laugh was the fact that DG just stayed in the cupboard for about a minute before he chose to come out again. He must have realised very quickly that he was in a cupboard, and in particular that he was in the dark because there was no light in there. And yet he didn't immediately turn around and come back into the room. What was his thought process? How else was he going to get out of the cupboard than through the door that he entered it? It was the delay in his return to the room that tipped me over the edge. DG was in the cupboard with no way of saving face and having to resign himself to making an undignified return to the room that he had stormed out of in such a theatrical huff.

I got the giggles, and Tarquin got the giggles because I got the giggles. Within a few seconds, even though wounded by the indignity that he'd suffered, DG and Tarquin and I were rolling around helpless with laughter. It was very funny.

Over the next couple of years we went on to sell project after project that Tarquin was building to investors who were based in the South of England. These were new-build blocks of flats, all valued highly at the time, but unfortunately as we later discovered the values were going to take a pounding in the 2008 crash.

I have to say that I for one embraced the opportunity to sell new build properties. They were clean, shiny and new. We had smart brochures printed and I took pride in presenting them to investors, because they were well built and they were sensibly sized. Tarquin did a great job.

They were also located in very strong residential areas, and growing up in the South of England we were quite accustomed to the idea of people living in flats. It was part of our culture and so selling new builds got us away from selling grubby little Victorian terraced properties. At least that is how I saw it at the time.

The structure of the deal was as follows. He would decide the total amount of money that he wanted to bring in for each development and this would be based on his costs and his required margin. Anything that we could get over and above that global figure across the development as a whole, he was happy for us to keep as our fee. You will understand that this was a significant incentive to us and in developments where there were nine or sometimes 12 flats available to sell, we could sometimes realise total fees in the region of £70,000-£80,000 just by selling the flats to existing investors. So that is what we did. This is one of the developments, pictured below.

Chapter Thirty:
Just Flippin' Do It

You have now come to the end of my book, but is this just the beginning of your property career?

In my experience, so many people started out with tentative steps into the world of property and just a few years later have found that it has transformed their lives and fortunes. You can do that too. You are just a few steps away from putting yourself and your family on the road to building lasting wealth.

You have read my book and I am honoured that you have stuck with me and are still here right at the end. I feel it is my responsibility to make sure that you actually use the knowledge that you've picked up in the book and that you launch your journey into property.

The most important thing is to find a network of people who can help you and support you, as this is a people business. Property isn't about the houses or the flats or the offices. It is about the people who can help you and guide you on your way. If you've taken anything from my story in this book then I hope you've seen that at every stage I was only able to move forwards because of the people I had around me and the new people that I met along the way. The one thing that changed my property life and moved me forward in the shortest amount of time was finding a community of like-minded people who could help and support me. In my case, it was the Progressive Property community that gave me the sounding board and the support to move forward to build lasting wealth.

I am going to give you a list of actionable steps that you can take today to get you started on your way, and it is important that you start today. Do it now while everything is fresh in your mind and hopefully, while you are feeling energised and excited having read the book, in the realisation that you can do it.

It is not difficult to do but you do have to take action and do it.

Here is what you should do now:

1. **Go and meet some Estate Agents.** Practice your scripts and what you are going to say to them. If you are nervous that you haven't nailed down your scripts at this time, then a very good piece of advice is to go to the next town, away from where you actually intend to invest and start to practice on estate agents there. We will know that you are not intending to buy there, but they don't. Pretend it's real and go through the steps as if it was real. It is the best practice you will get.

2. **Find yourself a great mortgage broker.** They are out there and you need one. Where can you find one? Well get yourself into a supportive property community who will know where you can go. I am a member of the Progressive Property Investors Community on Facebook and there are over 20,000 positive, supportive members in that group. They are doing it already and they will recommend brokers to you as well as anyone else that you need in your new property business.

3. **Find yourself a great property solicitor.** Again, if you join the Progressive community, they will short circuit the search for you and you can be set up within the hour.

4. **Have lunch with someone you know who has cash.** Tell them about your plans and dreams and about your new property business. You may be surprised at how supportive they will be.

5. **Find yourself a local property network meeting and go to it.** These are two separate action steps. You have to go to the meeting, and the magic happens only if you go. There are Progressive Property Network meetings all over the country where you can meet likeminded people on the same journey as you. If you go to progressivepropertynetwork. co.uk then you can find your nearest meeting.

6. **Do not procrastinate.** Procrastination will kill you. Be reassured, it's not only you who procrastinates and we all have to struggle with it every day. I have struggled with procrastination while I writing this book. Having read this book, you will hopefully now be feeling excited, energised, committed and ready to start your new life. If you don't start now, but instead put it off until who-knows-when, then all the enthusiasm and drive and excitement will fade away and a month from now you may have forgotten all about it. Now is the time! It is fate! It was in the stars that I wrote this book now – I have never written a book before – and then you have found it and it has triggered in you the passion to build a great property portfolio and a legacy for yourself and your family. Seize the moment. Just flippin' do it.

7. **Do not make the same old excuses to yourself.** "I don't have the money." "I don't have the time." "I don't know where to start." "What if it all goes wrong?" "Is it the right time?" Just realise that none of these excuses can stop you; it is a people business. All you need to do is surround yourself with the right people and they will help and guide you. They will elegantly keep you on the straight and narrow and your success will be assured.

8. **Realise that there is never going to be a "right" time to start.** All you can do is your best, but also realise that it is much better to start now than never to start at all. In just a short amount of time you will be able to look back and be so glad that you started today.

9. **You will make mistakes.** We all do. The important thing is to have the right advice and help around you so that you can fix any mistakes and move forward. Join the Progressive community and put your fears, concerns and shouts for help out there.

10. **Get yourself a mentor, someone who has been there, done it, knows how to do it, and can help you move forward on your property adventure.** "Don't wait to buy property, buy property and wait", so said one of my mentors Mark Homer, one of the smartest people in property that I have ever met. When I was a young man I had another mentor in my life and his message was also valuable and as true today as it was then. He said "Success in property David, is as easy as falling off a log. The secret is to stay on the log long enough". Make a start today. In one year from now you will be on your way. In five years from now your life and finances will be in a completely different place. In ten years' time you will not even recognise yourself.

I look forward to seeing you on the journey.

David Siegler